The Incredible Incas
and Their Timeless Land

By Loren McIntyre   Photographs by the Author

Paintings by Louis S. Glanzman
Foreword by Peruvian Historian Eugenio Alarco

Prepared by the Special Publications Division,
National Geographic Society, Washington, D. C.

THE INCREDIBLE INCAS
AND THEIR TIMELESS LAND
By LOREN MCINTYRE
Photographs by the Author
Paintings by LOUIS S. GLANZMAN

Published by
THE NATIONAL GEOGRAPHIC SOCIETY
ROBERT E. DOYLE, President
MELVIN M. PAYNE, Chairman of the Board
GILBERT M. GROSVENOR, Editor
MELVILLE BELL GROSVENOR, Editor Emeritus

Prepared by
THE SPECIAL PUBLICATIONS DIVISION
ROBERT L. BREEDEN, Editor
DONALD J. CRUMP, Associate Editor
PHILIP B. SILCOTT, Senior Editor
ROBERT PAUL JORDAN, Managing Editor
WILLIAM R. GRAY, Assistant Managing Editor
TONI EUGENE, BARBARA GRAZZINI, SALLIE M.
    GREENWOOD, SUE SHELTON MCINTYRE, Research
DOROTHY MENZEL, PH.D., Consultant, Associate
    Research Anthropologist, University of California,
    Berkeley
JOHN HEMMING, Consultant, Director of the Royal
    Geographical Society

Illustrations
DAVID R. BRIDGE, Picture Editor
MARJORIE W. CLINE, Illustrations Research
WILLIAM R. GRAY, P. TYRUS HARRINGTON,
    MARGARET MCKELWAY, TOM MELHAM, TEE
    LOFTIN, MARILYN L. WILBUR, Picture Legends

Design and Art Direction
JOSEPH A. TANEY, Staff Art Director
JOSEPHINE B. BOLT, Art Director
URSULA PERRIN, Assistant Art Director
JOHN D. GARST, JR., MARGARET A. DEANE, TIBOR
    G. TOTH, NANCY SCHWEICKART, ALFRED L.
    ZEBARTH, Map Research, Design, and Production

Production and Printing
ROBERT W. MESSER, Production Manager
GEORGE V. WHITE, Assistant Production Manager
RAJA D. MURSHED, JUNE L. GRAHAM, Production
    Assistants
JOHN R. METCALFE, Engraving and Printing
MARY G. BURNS, JANE H. BUXTON, STEPHANIE
    S. COOKE, SUZANNE J. JACOBSON, SANDRA LEE
    MATTHEWS, SELINA PATTON, MARILYN L.
    WILBUR, KAREN G. WILSON, LINDA M. YEE,
    Staff Assistants
VIRGINIA S. THOMPSON, PHILIP
    G. GUTEKUNST, Index

*Ears perked, a day-old llama stands on
wobbly legs in a meadow high in the
21,000-foot Royal Range of Bolivia.
Llamas carried supplies for conquering Inca armies into all corners of their
empire, known as Tahuantinsuyu—the
Four Quarters of the World. The Incas
tenaciously controlled this vast realm,
imposing their language, law, and religion on almost one hundred nations.*

*Overleaf: Relaying a memorized message, a youthful chasqui
—post runner—speeds along a stone road in the Andes. Page 1:
A silver figurine of a goddess, buried as an offering to the
gods, wears a crown of bird feathers. Bookbinding: Gold llama
found in a tomb near 12,500-foot-high Lake Titicaca in Peru.*

PAGE 1: NATURAL HISTORY MUSEUM, SANTIAGO; BOOKBINDING: MUSEUM AND
INSTITUTE OF ARCHEOLOGY, UNIVERSITY OF SAN ANTONIO ABAD, CUZCO

Foreword

AT HOME in Lima, Peru, I go into my study every day, open a volume of history, and lose myself in reflections about other ages. At such times, I have studied and written about ancient Peru, impressed by the arts and accomplishments of early cultures as well as the magnitude and grandeur of the Inca Empire.

I marvel at the sweep of lands the Incas overran—mountains, jungle, coastal deserts—and at the diversity of nations they welded into a unified state. I admire the Incas' splendid craftsmanship—particularly their monumental works in stone. Their cunning in war and administrative power in peace were astonishing.

For years I have surveyed this unique American Indian empire that had its genesis in a secluded mountain valley high in the Andes of Peru. From that small beginning, the Incas embarked on conquests that gave them dominion over an immense area in western South America. My studies have also focused on another equally great people, the Spaniards, who succeeded in bringing down the Inca Empire. The intermingled descendants of the Incas and the Spaniards now constitute the dominant population of Peru.

During my research work I encountered an enthusiastic Inca scholar, Loren McIntyre. Mac is author and photographer of this book—and a good friend. He has lived and worked since 1947 in all the Andean countries where the Incas left their stamp: Peru, Bolivia, Ecuador, Colombia, Chile, Argentina.

He and I have spent enjoyable evenings talking about Inca culture, history, and religion. We have discussed early chroniclers who erroneously recorded that the Inca nation emerged at the height of its power from a land inhabited by scattered, backward peoples. We have delved into modern writings, based mainly on archeological findings, that reveal several millenniums of development which culminated with the Inca civilization.

As a result of our talks, I have come to know Mac as a dedicated reporter and scholar and as a lively storyteller. Members of the National Geographic Society know from his magazine articles that he is an excellent photographer and writer.

In this book he combines his talents to produce an exciting, compelling, and informative account of the Inca Empire. He has synthesized legend with scientific evidence and has interwoven history with personal experience. The result brings the Incas to life once again.

Now I am pleased to add this fine volume to my bookshelves.

EUGENIO ALARCO
Recipient of Inca Garcilaso Award
National Institute of Culture, Peru

Contents

Festive Spanish dress and Inca surname of Peruvian highlander Hilda Guanaco reflect the heritage of both the Incas and Spaniards.

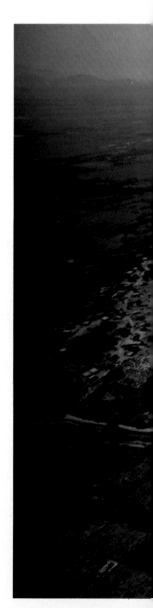

CHAPTER ONE

WARRIOR OF STONE AND SHELL EMBELLISHES
THREE-INCH GOLD EAR CAP. MUJICA GALLO
MUSEUM, LIMA, PERU

The Silent

GOLD, TO THE INCAS, was "the sweat of the sun," and silver "the tears of the moon."

Their love of precious metals was esthetic, for neither Incas nor their subjects needed to buy anything. Six million or more worshipful people rendered abundant tribute to the Incas and paid their taxes in work: a billion man-hours a year to build temples, fortresses, agricultural terraces, and roads — all for the grandeur of the realm.

"The riches that were gathered in the city of Cuzco alone, as capital and court of the Empire, were incredible," a priest penned more than three centuries ago, "for therein were many palaces of dead kings with all the treasure that each amassed in life; and he who began to reign did not touch the estate and wealth of his predecessor but ... built a new palace and acquired for himself silver and gold and all the rest. ..."

I learned of the priest's writings from a friend, archeologist John Howland Rowe, whom I first met one day as he pored over potsherds in Cuzco, high in the Andes of southern Peru. In John's words: "Of all works, ancient or modern, the *Historia del Nuevo Mundo* by the Jesuit Father Bernabé Cobo ... is still the best and most complete description of Inca culture in existence."

Father Cobo wrote that Cuzco became the richest city in the New World. Chiefs and governors, he said, made presents to the Inca when they visited his court and when he went to their lands while touring his kingdom. This wealth grew daily, for provinces were many and others were continually being brought to obedience.

It was prohibited to remove silver and gold from Cuzco. "Nor was it spent," recorded Father Cobo "in things that are consumed with use," but for idols, goblets, and ornaments for the temples, the king, and great nobles. As money did not exist, rulers paid their retainers in clothing and food.

Gold was the undoing of the Incas, for it excited merciless greed in the Spaniards, who had mainly been looking for shorter spice routes when they chanced upon the New World. Indians hid gold when they saw with what avarice Spaniards sought it. The

Strings

Plundered temples and tombs—ruins of El Purgatorio, a ceremonial center of the Kingdom of Chimor—ring a rocky outcropping on Peru's north coast. Inca armies conquered this desert nation in the mid-1400's, incorporating it into the expanding empire. Centuries of erosion and looting that followed the Spanish conquest have left the complex in rubble.

Overleaf: Royal procession brings the Governor of Antisuyu—one of the Inca Empire's Four Quarters of the World—to Cuzco along Jatun Rumiyoc, the street of the big stones. Each May officials journeyed to the capital to present reports and tribute to the emperor. More than 500 years ago, Indians carved and fitted huge rocks to form the street and the walls of temples and palaces; many stand firmly even today.

search for hidden treasure goes on to this day. In Peru, I have photographed hundreds of pillaged tombs and graveyards that from a low-flying aircraft appeared to be shell-cratered battlefields. In Ecuador, when I descended from the summit of 19,347-foot Cotopaxi, one of the world's loftiest volcanoes, suspicious villagers asked whether I had found Inca gold in the steaming crater.

My fascination with the lost world of the Incas goes back to boyhood days. Among worn volumes of adventure in my grandfather's bookcase, I discovered a story about the incredible Incas; it cast upon me a spell unbroken now for almost half a century. On long winter nights I used to read and reread the *History of the Conquest of Peru* by flashlight under the bedclothes while my parents supposed I was asleep. Author William H. Prescott's account of imperial splendor persuaded me that life among the Incas—even to taking a bath—was the epitome of pleasure.

The Incas, Prescott wrote, "loved to retreat, and solace themselves with the society of their favorite concubines, wandering amidst groves and airy gardens, that shed around their soft, intoxicating odors and lulled the senses to voluptuous repose. Here, too, they loved to indulge in the luxury of their baths, replenished by streams of crystal water which were conducted through subterraneous silver channels into basins of gold."

In years to come, I never saw the silver channels or gold basins, and almost every Inca bath I put my toe into was icy cold. But I could not blame Prescott for leading me into imaginary gardens of delight, for most of what the near-blind Bostonian scholar wrote is true. Having gained access to chronicles newly exhumed from archives in Spain, he became the first to publish, in 1847, a thorough and well-written English-language account of the splendor and tragedy of the Inca Empire.

That empire dawned about 1438, shortly before the birth of Columbus, when the Incas strode forth from Cuzco to conquer the world around them on a scale worthy of Caesar's envy. Cuzco was then a minor agricultural state on an Amazon tributary in the Peruvian Andes. The forge of empire roared in the person of the emperor Pachacuti, ninth in the dynasty of Incas, lords of Cuzco. His name means "cataclysm" or "he who transforms the earth."

By the time Columbus set sail, Pachacuti and his son Tupa Inca had created an unprecedented universal state—without benefit of money, iron, the written word, or the wheel. And yet the Incas impressed their rule, their law, their religion, and even their highland tongue, Quechua, on almost a hundred nations whose peoples' lives they regulated to the last detail. They called their empire Tahuantinsuyu, the Four Quarters of the World. At its peak, it stretched 2,500 miles from central Chile into southern Colombia.

All who inhabited Tahuantinsuyu are termed Incas nowadays,

although in olden times the title Inca applied only to the royal family, whose men wore huge earplugs. Taxing their subjects and exacting tribute from wealthy states, a succession of Incas amassed enormous treasure which they lavished on Cuzco.

Rumors of the city of gold lured adventurers following in the wake of Columbus. Finally, in 1532, Francisco Pizarro led a small band of Spaniards into the Inca Empire. The invaders fell upon the reigning Inca, Atahuallpa, and his people at a time when the empire had been scourged by plague and civil war. With astonishing feats of courage and cruelty, the conquistadors overran the weakened dominion and made off with shiploads of booty.

When word of Pizarro's exploits and reports of other hidden realms of riches reached Europe, treasure seekers thronged into the Spanish ports, vying for passage to the New World. Others, however, were angered by the Incas' tragic fate. The King of Spain voiced displeasure at the execution of the ruler Atahuallpa, "since he was a monarch, and particularly as it was done in the name of justice...." Later in the century the French essayist Montaigne, looking back on the conquest, lamented that "the richest, the fairest and the best part of the world [was] topsyturvied, ruined...."

Many Europeans had been spellbound by tales of the Incas' idyllic rule in their days of grandeur. One of the more fascinating spellbinders was Garcilaso de la Vega, who used more than 700,000 words to tell his story of the Inca Empire's rise and fall. The first great chronicler born in the New World, in 1539, "El Inca" Garcilaso was the son of a conquistador and an Inca princess who was the emperor Pachacuti's great-granddaughter. At 20, Garcilaso left his native Cuzco for Spain. He fought in Mediterranean wars, took religious vows, and wrote in his old age. He died in 1616.

A man of good will, Garcilaso admired his Inca and Spanish forebears and eulogized both cultures in his picturesque history, which was largely fanciful except for remembrances of his boyhood in Cuzco. He related a legend of Inca origins learned at the knee of his royal uncle: how all the land was desolate mountains, and people lived in grottoes like beasts, eating grass and roots and even human flesh, going naked or covering themselves with skins. And how, seeing their miserable condition, the Sun sent his son and daughter to walk the wilderness and teach mankind to live in houses, work the soil, raise llamas, and enjoy the fruits of the earth.

Since first reading Garcilaso, I have learned that his royal uncle overlooked a few millenniums in his oral history. Thousands of years before the Incas appeared, hunters and gatherers discovered how to cultivate cereals and tubers and became attached to the land. By Old Testament times, communities had risen. While Christianity was transforming Europe, other religions helped to shape the growth of civilization in the coastal oases and highland valleys of western South America.

I first saw the Pacific Coast of South America as the conquistador Pizarro beheld it: from a vessel out of Panama, southbound over abysmal deeps hard by a lifeless shore. First came jungled slopes, then mangrove swamps, and finally barren dunes cooled by an ocean current flowing north from Antarctic seas. I know of no record that thunder, lightning, hail, snow, or tempest has

Artwork from the tombs of pre-Inca civilizations illuminates their cultures. Embroidered figure (left) emblazons the cloak of a 2,000-year-old mummy found at Paracas, south of Lima, Peru. Paracas artisans—masters at weaving, knitting, and decorating textiles—created some of the finest fabrics in the New World. Their bright, imaginative designs often portrayed vital features of daily life: gods, chieftains, women, and wildlife. Textiles also dominated the art of the Chancay peoples north of Lima. Here, prolific embroiderers, lacemakers, and weavers worked in a rich variety of styles and hues, both before and during the rise of the Incas. A 14th-century tunic (below left) blazes with color; a fabric house (bottom) shelters male and female figures. Chancay burial sites still yield such woven offerings. On the north coast of Peru, the first-millennium Mochica civilization produced pyramids, polychrome murals, and gold jewelry as well as fabrics. Pottery, however, remains its most notable achievement. A realistic "portrait vessel" (right), cast from a mold, shows the features of a warrior, a chief, or a priest.

ever assailed this coast in all the 1,400 miles from Ecuador to Chile. A brief shower once or twice in a lifetime is the rule.

For ten years my wife, Sue, and I made our home on Avenida Los Incas in a suburb of Lima, Peru, the capital that Pizarro founded near the sea. Our neighbors and inhabitants of other coastal urban clusters were largely Caucasian and Hispanic in culture, mixed with a measure of Indian, if not Inca, ancestry.

But Inca traditions survive — perpetuated by rote learning — even on the coast, as I found when our six-year-old son Lance returned from his first day at school. He stomped through the house chanting "Manco Capac, Sinchi Roca, Lloque Yupanqui, Mayta Capac, Capac Yupanqui, Inca Roca, Yahuar Huacac, Viracocha, Pachacuti, Tupa Inca Yupanqui, Huayna Capac, Huascar, Atahuallpa." To this day, Peruvian schoolchildren recite in one long breath the singsong names of the Inca dynasty.*

Four blocks from our home towered an adobe temple, proof of an earlier civilization whose existence the Incas had denied when they claimed to be the first civilizers of a savage land. Lance and our other son, Scott, used to scamper up the parapets of a temple three times as tall as the olive trees around it and a city block in length. Like priests a thousand years before the Incas, the boys could see east to the Andes and west to the Pacific Ocean.

This quadrilateral pyramid was one of thousands of coastal Peruvian *huacas* — Quechua for "holy places or things" — built in irrigated oases by rich, independent states that emerged before the time of Christ. The largest adobe huaca contained more than 140 million bricks. Extreme aridity helped preserve such earthen temples, as well as tombs, mummies, jewels, ceramics, and garments. More than a million relics have ended up in the world's museums and private collections despite the disdain of grave robbers at first for everything except gold, silver, and gems. Smashed potsherds and human bones are strewn over vast areas of Peruvian coastal desert. Countless adobe ruins have been plowed under to plant cotton. Power shovels obliterated my children's pre-Inca temple playground long ago, leveling the block for modern homes.

In 1957 we moved to Bolivia, where rural highlanders are largely pure-blooded Indian and, in secluded places, hardly changed since Inca times. For six years we lived in the oxygen-thin air of La Paz, whose elevation measures 11,900 feet at the city's center. Occasionally we dropped down to Lima for "altitude relief."

We would take several days to drive back up from Lima to La Paz, a distance of 1,100 miles by way of Cuzco. We followed the Pan American Highway along the coast, paralleling traces of Inca post roads. Spanish chronicler Pedro de Cieza de León, who soldiered thousands of miles from the Caribbean coast to Bolivia, judged Inca thoroughfares to be the world's finest. Of one he wrote:

". . . In the memory of man, no highway is as great as this, laid through deep valleys and over high mountains, through snowbanks and quagmires, through live rock and along raging rivers; in some places smooth and paved, in others tunneled through cliffs, skirting gorges, linking snow peaks with stairways and rest stops; everywhere clean-swept and litter-free, with lodgings, storehouses, and temples of the sun. . . . (Continued on page 22)

*A chart of the Inca dynasty and a pronunciation guide appear on page 199.

Millions of seabirds (above) nested on Peru's offshore islands as recently as the 1960's, thriving on anchovy that abounded in chill ocean currents. Peoples of ancient coastal civilizations gathered the birds' guano —layered to a depth of 150 feet—to enrich the sandy soil of their lands and improve the production of crops. Today, overfishing and changing currents have depleted the anchovy, and few birds survive (below).

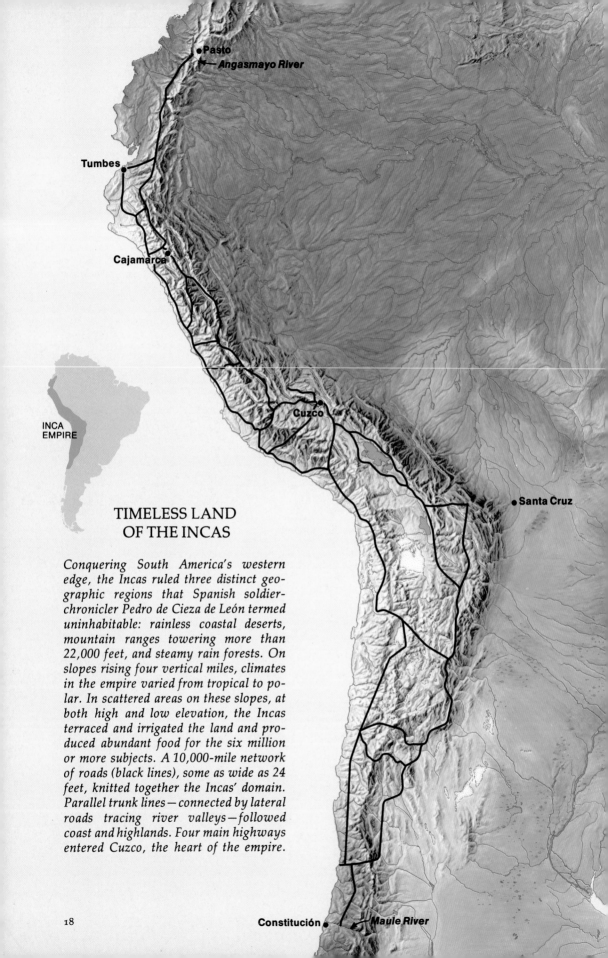

Pasto
Angasmayo River

Tumbes

Cajamarca

INCA
EMPIRE

Cuzco

Santa Cruz

TIMELESS LAND
OF THE INCAS

Conquering South America's western edge, the Incas ruled three distinct geographic regions that Spanish soldier-chronicler Pedro de Cieza de León termed uninhabitable: rainless coastal deserts, mountain ranges towering more than 22,000 feet, and steamy rain forests. On slopes rising four vertical miles, climates in the empire varied from tropical to polar. In scattered areas on these slopes, at both high and low elevation, the Incas terraced and irrigated the land and produced abundant food for the six million or more subjects. A 10,000-mile network of roads (black lines), some as wide as 24 feet, knitted together the Incas' domain. Parallel trunk lines—connected by lateral roads tracing river valleys—followed coast and highlands. Four main highways entered Cuzco, the heart of the empire.

Constitución
Maule River

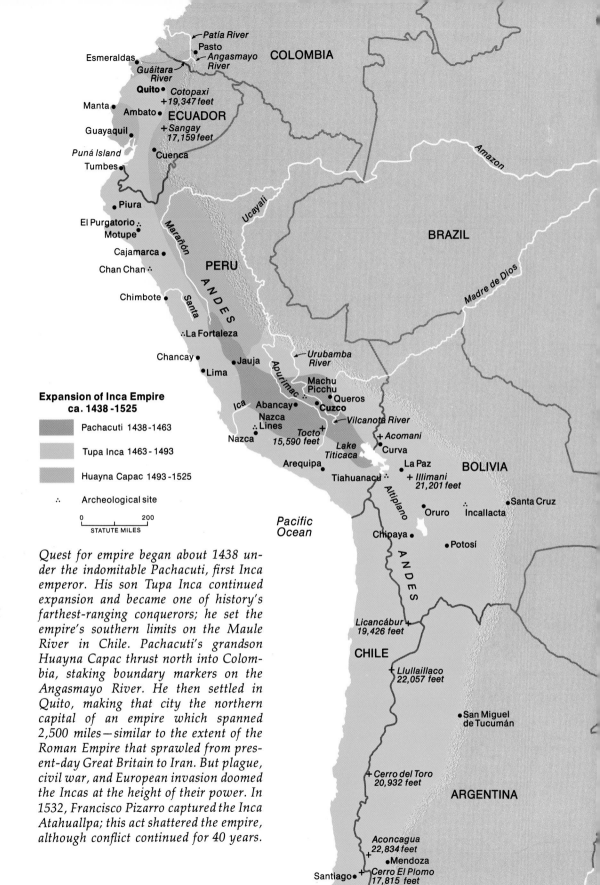

Patía River
Pasto
Angasmayo River
COLOMBIA
Esmeraldas
Guáitara River
Quito
Cotopaxi +19,347 feet
Manta
Ambato
ECUADOR
+Sangay 17,159 feet
Guayaquil
Puná Island
Cuenca
Tumbes
Piura
El Purgatorio
Motupe
Marañón
Cajamarca
Chan Chan
PERU
ANDES
Chimbote
Santa
La Fortaleza
Chancay
Jauja
Urubamba River
Lima
Apurímac
Machu Picchu
Ica
Abancay
Queros
Cuzco
Nazca Lines
Vilcanota River
Nazca
Tocto 15,590 feet
+Acomani
Lake Titicaca
Curva
Arequipa
La Paz
BOLIVIA
Tiahuanaco
+Illimani 21,201 feet
Altiplano
Santa Cruz
Oruro
Incallacta
Chipaya
Potosí
Pacific Ocean

Ucayali
BRAZIL
Amazon
Madre de Dios

ANDES

Licancábur 19,426 feet
CHILE
+Llullaillaco 22,057 feet
San Miguel de Tucumán
+Cerro del Toro 20,932 feet
ARGENTINA
Aconcagua +22,834 feet
Mendoza
Santiago
+Cerro El Plomo 17,815 feet
Constitución
Maule

Expansion of Inca Empire ca. 1438 -1525

Pachacuti 1438 -1463

Tupa Inca 1463 - 1493

Huayna Capac 1493 -1525

∴ Archeological site

0 ────── 200
STATUTE MILES

Quest for empire began about 1438 under the indomitable Pachacuti, first Inca emperor. His son Tupa Inca continued expansion and became one of history's farthest-ranging conquerors; he set the empire's southern limits on the Maule River in Chile. Pachacuti's grandson Huayna Capac thrust north into Colombia, staking boundary markers on the Angasmayo River. He then settled in Quito, making that city the northern capital of an empire which spanned 2,500 miles—similar to the extent of the Roman Empire that sprawled from present-day Great Britain to Iran. But plague, civil war, and European invasion doomed the Incas at the height of their power. In 1532, Francisco Pizarro captured the Inca Atahuallpa; this act shattered the empire, although conflict continued for 40 years.

Legendary birthplace of the first Inca, Lake Titicaca's Island of the Sun even today provides a stage for sacrificial Inca-style ceremonies. Resident Aymara Indians start their annual planting celebration in morning sun, when an islander (below) paddles a reed boat to the mainland and returns with a white llama. Sorcerers (left) prepare bread, flowers, and other offerings that the animal will wear on its back in a charm bundle. Behind them, women sit with piles of coca leaves, used to divine the most propitious sacrificial site on the island. Swirling skirts in the background reflect the revelry that will fill the day: dancing, the music of panpipes, and copious drinking. At dusk, several men hold down the streamer-draped llama as another severs its jugular vein; some drink the blood, others scatter it on Pacha Mama—Earth Mother. Burning of incense (below left) to assuage the evil spirit that controls frost, hail, and lightning completes the ceremony; islanders then feast on their sacrificial offering as in Inca days.

"Oh, can such grandeur be said of Alexander or any of the mighty kings who ruled the world, that they built such a road or provided the supplies found on this one? The Roman road through Spain and the others we read of were as nothing compared to this."

Of a dozen chronicles I have read in Spanish, I carried only Cieza's account on my travels. A native of Extremadura, the 13-year-old Cieza was in Seville early in 1534 when treasure galleons unloaded Pizarro's first great shipments from Peru. What he saw fired his imagination—jar after golden jar, bars of gold and silver, and even an intricately-wrought golden fountain. Months later, the boy sailed for South America. There, for 17 years, he campaigned in Colombia and in the stricken Inca Empire.

Around 20, he took up his quill. He was concerned, as he later wrote to King Philip, that ". . . not only admirable deeds of many and very brave men, but also countless things deserving to be remembered forever of great and varied regions, have remained in the dark night of forgetfulness for lack of writers. . . ." While other soldiers rested, "I wearied myself with writing," he recalled.

True soldier-writers are rare in any age. Cieza's accomplishment, in the midst of cruel struggles and constant dangers, was extraordinary. At a time when a clean sheet of paper was very hard to come by, he filled his saddlebags with carefully written reams of history and more knowledgeable geography of Indian regions than in many a modern textbook.

Cieza reported that the wars had sadly depopulated the occasional irrigated valleys crossing the strip of coastal sand between mountains and sea. Driving through these same lowlands on our travels out of Lima, homeward bound for La Paz, we usually spent the first night at Nazca, in the southern coastal desert. The town's name is associated with an ancient civilization that produced sophisticated painted pottery and the famed Nazca Lines, mysterious patterns traced on a desert plateau, some in the form of birds and animals and some looking like airport runways.

The second day we turned eastward. Grinding up a gravel road in low gear for hours to cross a 15,000-foot-high plateau, we picked up the alternate Panamericana that follows the crest of the Andes. Then we dropped into the awesome gorge of the Apurimac River which cut Cuzco off from the Inca Empire's western reaches.

Emerging from the gorge on the Cuzco side, we drove past Tarahuasi, an abandoned Inca ceremonial center, and sighted fragments of stone highways and causeways. Over them, armies used to march with supply trains of llamas, the beasts of burden that contributed to Inca military might. We would pass the second night or two in Cuzco among cold ruins and warm friends—like John Rowe, who spends his summers probing the city's origins. I regard John as the world's leading expert on the Incas. For more than a quarter of a century, his research has helped me weed

Ancient Nazca Line—made by clearing away rocks and exposing the lighter-colored ground—etches the nearly rainless coastal plateau of southern Peru. Archeologists attribute this and other mysterious markings, some in the shape of birds and animals, to the desert Nazca culture that flourished perhaps 1,000 years before the rise of the Inca Empire.

Deer adorn a Chimu
religious vessel

Inca jug possibly
held holy drink

Chimu necklace
of gold and pearl

GOLD: fiery metal esteemed by the Incas
for its beauty and sought by the Spaniards
for its worth. Exciting the greed of conquistadors, it brought an empire to ruin. To
the Incas, gold was "the sweat of the sun,"
and it reflected the glory of their Sun God
who, they believed, had entrusted them
with its safekeeping. Gold took on value
only when crafted into ceremonial articles
—vessels, jewelry, figurines—or adorn-
ments for tombs and temples. By law, all
gold and silver of the realm belonged to
the emperor, who used it to bedeck his
palace, beautify temples, and reward
loyalty. Most gold—in the form of nuggets
and flakes—came from mountain rivers;
Incas smelted the ore with charcoal and
bellows. They learned much of the craft
from artisans of the Chimu Kingdom, who
created countless vessels and ornaments.
Spaniards reduced such works of art into
ingots, easy to transport and exchange.

MUSEUM AND INSTITUTE OF ARCHEOLOGY, UNIVERSITY OF SAN ANTONIO
ABAD, CUZCO (JUG AND FIGURINE); MUJICA GALLO MUSEUM, LIMA

Gold hands and arms
sheathed Chimu mummy

Rare Inca figurine
—ten inches high

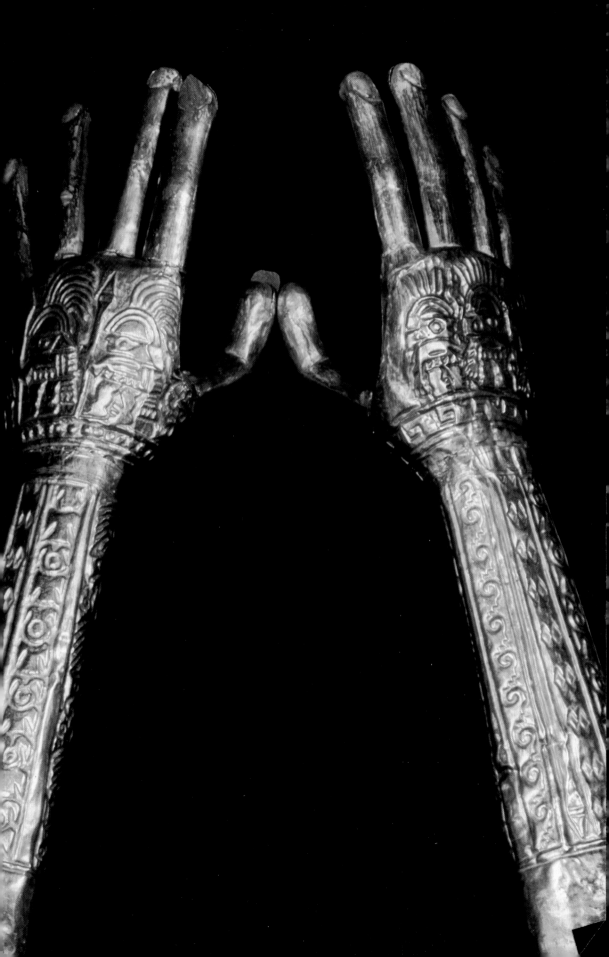

nonsense from Andean reality. "We've traced man's presence in Cuzco back to 600 B.C., at least 1,800 years before the Incas," John once told us. And he taught us how to distinguish Inca ruins from those of earlier and later cultures.

Heading southeast from Cuzco to Lake Titicaca, we covered 240 miles on the next leg of our journey. But we invariably arrived after dark no matter how early we set out. We desired, like Cieza, to seek out and explore byways. Roads branching into the mountains on either side of the highway often led to Inca enclaves or to landscapes utterly pristine—except for a lone farmer, now and then, toiling on an ancient terrace.

Passersby who fail to turn a quarter-mile off the highway will miss the ruins at Rajchi, near San Pedro, 75 miles out of Cuzco. A great stone wall several miles long borders acres of terraces, numerous two-story dwellings, scores of storehouses, a highway of black volcanic rock polished by centuries of plodding feet, and the remains of a temple 303 feet long, 87 feet wide, and 40 feet high. One of the biggest buildings the Incas constructed, the temple was dedicated to Viracocha, their supreme being.

The Incas believed that Viracocha created men and women in his own image at Tiahuanacu, near the southern shore of Lake Titicaca. He gave them tribal customs and languages and sent them into the earth with orders to emerge from certain caves, lakes, and hills to make settlements. The ancients worshiped their places of origin. Many highland dwellers revere them today.

After the creation, Viracocha walked northwest from Titicaca, appearing as an old white man carrying a staff. He taught mankind how to live. People at Rajchi stoned the stranger. He called down fire from heaven which burned a nearby hill, subduing them. In fact, the Rajchi temple region was bombarded in prehistoric times with lumps of lava from a small volcano nearby.

Viracocha then proceeded north to the Pacific Coast near present-day Manta, Ecuador, where he bade mankind farewell and set off across the ocean walking on the water. The Incas believed that he would return in times of crisis.

Southeast of Viracocha's temple, the highway threads Inca Empire homeland—where scores of other intriguing ruins lie just out of sight—all the way to Lake Titicaca, which Bolivia and Peru share. On our first drive to La Paz, Sue and I arrived late at a stone jetty on the lake to find the Indian ferryboat crew sailing away in the dark. We were only two hours short of our destination.

Parked on the jetty that bitterly cold night, we huddled in the car. Moonlight glittered on the Strait of Tiquina, near the southeastern end of the 12,500-foot-high lake. We had company. Hundreds of human shapes lay rolled up in ponchos on the rocky beach. Some rose, and soon dozens of faces pressed against our windows. We got out, locked the car, and pushed our way through muffled figures to a small hotel on a hill. Its dim halls were packed with travelers complaining in Spanish and Aymara, the language

World's loftiest capital city, La Paz lines a canyon cut into Bolivia's 13,500-foot altiplano by an Amazon tributary. The Incas seized this region in the mid-1400's; a century later Spaniards founded the city.

of about a million highland Indians around the Lake Titicaca region of both Peru and Bolivia.

"Pilgrims," the innkeeper explained. "It is Holy Week." No rooms were available at this resting place between La Paz and a lakeshore mecca, Copacabana—the Place Where the Jewel Can Be Seen. In their prayers for a great favor, such as the recovery of a loved one, pilgrims promise the Virgin of Copacabana that they will walk the hundred miles from La Paz—some on their knees—to her shrine.

Escaping to a secluded hillside, Sue and I shivered all night in a graveyard overlooking Lake Titicaca, watching the wind pick up blossoms from withered wreaths and scatter them among the adobe tombs. We decided that in the future we would drive around the southern end of the lake, passing close by Tiahuanacu. The Incas believed that massive carved stone monoliths at Tiahuanacu's huge ceremonial center were left over from Viracocha's attempts to create a race of giants while the world was still in darkness. This shrine attracted pilgrims from afar in pre-Inca times when Cuzco was hardly more than a village.

When day broke, we crossed the strait under sail and then sped over the undulating altiplano toward the highest seat of government in the world. In winter sunshine, in summer hailstorm, or on a chill starlit night, La Paz unveils a breathtaking view from the brink of the 13,500-foot altiplano. Its buildings cover the walls and floor of a chasm two miles wide and half a mile deep. A river which long ago scoured the canyon from the surrounding plateau now flows unseen through a tunnel beneath the city. Beyond the abyss the triple peaks of Illimani rise more than 21,000 feet. Off to the left the Cordillera Real—Royal Range—lifts a long rampart of perpetual snows between Lake Titicaca and the Amazon headwater jungle.

So many ancient ruins lie hidden in the rain forest which carpets the eastern slope of the Andes that hardly a year goes by without the discovery, or rediscovery, of another complex. Sweating modern explorers brave torrential downpours, voracious insects, and deadly bushmasters to free beautifully chiseled granite from 500 years of rank growth. The Incas bartered for bright ceremonial feathers and recruited bowmen from this cruel frontier, but they never fully absorbed the forest tribes into their Four Quarters of the World.

Often I have swung my hammock with jungle lowlanders whose way of life seemed to me small improvement over that of Stone Age nomads who migrated from Asia thousands of years ago. Those ancestors of the Incas wandered through the American continents hunting mastodons and gathering turtle eggs, tarrying, multiplying, and moving on until they reached land's end. In time, meltwater from subsiding ice broadened the seas, and waves erased the land that linked Asia with North America.

I have been initiated into the secret male lodges of several forest tribes, and have danced with them and heeded their taboos. Though the jungle people were not the first to arrive from the Old World, they are among the last to succumb to civilization, whether the Incas' or ours. Some still elude it.

Choked with vegetation and ridden with insects, snakes, and disease, the rain forests on the east side of the Andes barred Inca expansion. Fierce tribes, some of whom still evade civilization, also harassed the highland armies. In Ecuador, a boy rolls a cotton plug around a dart for his blowgun.

Andean highlander Mariano Quispe follows Inca ways—in customs, language, and even his record keeping. Using a quipu, a series of knotted strings, he tabulates crop and livestock production for each man in his hamlet. More elaborate quipus (right, top and bottom) served the Incas, whose culture lacked written numerals as well as the written word. With a decimal system, royal statisticians kept track of such vital data as births, deaths,

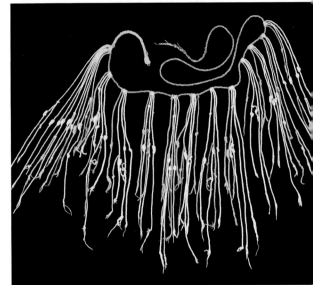

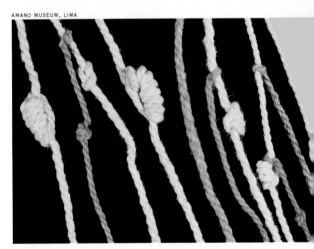

AMANO MUSEUM, LIMA

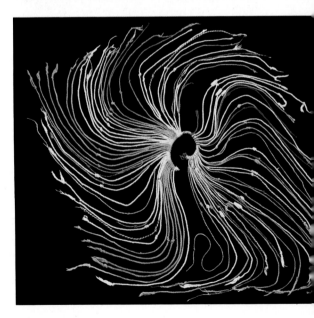

weapons, and food. Colors of yarn, knots, and the turns within a knot all related various information. A detail (middle) of a quipu shows the system's complexity. Each quipu-keeper might have hundreds of quipus coiled and stored in jars. But only professionally trained quipu "rememberers" could interpret the knots. Today, no one can tell what the silent strings recorded.

Over the years, despite the Incas' lack of a written language, the archives of their empire have been opened to me in many ways — by legend, oral tradition, archeology, and congenial ghosts: romantic Garcilaso writing in old age; keen-eyed Cieza carrying his inkpot into battle; colonial clerks and parish priests; William H. Prescott, the Bostonian who never saw the Peru he described so well. And by John Hemming, who did travel Peru and, in his book, *The Conquest of the Incas*, brought Prescott's history up to date with recently discovered chronicles.

And during my journeys, doors to learning were held wide by willing hands: scholarly John Rowe, assembling potsherd puzzles in Cuzco; the eminent Peruvian historian Eugenio Alarco, whose prize-winning history, *El Hombre Peruano en Su Historia*, guided me to rich sources of fact and fable; pilots and missionaries; and certain solemn Indians, dwelling on distant mountainsides like their forefathers, who offered me food and shelter.

I remember one Indian, Mariano Quispe, headman of Micay-pata. His hamlet lies over the mountains from Cuzco, several hours' hike beyond the highway. With his long hooked nose and leathery skin, Mariano looked like an Inca. He was beardless except for an occasional chin whisker that escaped bronze tweezers exactly like those found in Inca tombs.

I think of Mariano as the last of the *quipu camayocs*, those key rememberers who recorded Inca culture and history and kept statistical control of the empire. They relied on *quipus* — knotted strings often of different colors and lengths — to tally crops, llamas, weapons, births, and deaths. The rememberers explained to each other how their quipus were coded, so that the strings could be interpreted. The Incas used a decimal system and understood the abstract concept of zero. The invention of nothing, or zero, possibly occurred only three times in history: in India and from there through Arabia into Western culture, in the Maya civilization of Mexico, and in the Inca Empire.

Quipus were not used to compute but only to tally after totals were obtained with piles of grains or pebbles or by an abacuslike counting tray. Mariano showed me how he used colored lengths of yarn to represent the 18 men of his hamlet. To each different color he tied strings knotted according to each man's yearly production of corn, llamas, and loads of firewood. But without Mariano to remember and decode his personal choice of yarn and colors, and the things they counted, his quipu was meaningless to others. Does yellow signify gold . . . or merely corn?

Most museum quipus come from dry coastal graves; few highland quipus survive. At the end of a bloody civil war that shattered the realm just before the Europeans appeared, conquering generals burned the emperor's vast archive of quipus. Spaniards subsequently destroyed storerooms full of them to stamp out pagan practices and, suspecting idolatry, they even seized personal quipus.

Additional Inca quipus might turn up in a tomb some day, but such a find probably would be for naught. Who could tell whether the knots counted cornfields, sandals, llamas, virgins, huacas, mountains, or stars in the sky?

The rememberers are long dead, and the strings are silent.

The Sons

Rumpled ridges of the Island of the Sun rise above the waters of Lake Titicaca. Here, according to legend, the Sun God Inti created the first Incas; they wandered north, eventually founding the dynasty at Cuzco.

of the Sun

CHAPTER TWO

SOLID GOLD IDOLS FOUND IN CUZCO REFLECT
INCA NOBILITY. MUJICA GALLO MUSEUM, LIMA

"OH SUN, MY FATHER . . . let thy sons the Incas be conquerors and despoilers of all mankind. We adore thee and offer this sacrifice. . . ."

Thus the Incas prayed to the Sun, creator of their dynasty, according to Father Cobo, and ordered subject peoples to honor the Sun above all local gods. The dictum was easy for devout highlanders to accept. Almost anyone would adore the sun after spending a night two miles or more above sea level. Bone-biting cold descends in the Andes the moment the sun sets and — so the Incas believed — begins its nightlong swim beneath the earth.

On Lake Titicaca, whose waters friends and I used to troll for giant trout in a cabin cruiser, gales sweep down at dark from snows of the Royal Range. It was miserable to be caught at midnight bucking big waves out in the 3,200-square-mile lake.

I liked to anchor before dusk in a tall bed of *totora*, the reed used for making Inca-style boats. At dawn, when trout fishing was best, we were loath to leave our warm sleeping bags. Often I wiped condensation from a porthole and winced to see Aymara Indians, muffled to the ears, break a crust of ice at the water's edge with their bare feet. Then they would wade to their reed boats, pole out beyond the totora, and bait fishlines marked with wild geraniums tied to a bundle of floating reed.

The sun, bursting over the glaciered peaks, quickly banished the chill. Blood and sap quickened, ducks quacked overhead, red specks of ponchos moved across distant brown hills, and sails on unseen hulls poked over the curve of the horizon.

Soon a fireball glared from a cobalt sky and its image danced on the water. "Tie on that big straw hat," we'd warn a fair-skinned guest, "or you'll soon get badly burned." On Titicaca, the skin of an Aymara Indian looks like scorched leather.

Our trolling spoons caught the sun's rays and sent them darting through clear green water. Rainbow trout weighing 20 pounds attacked and made the reels zing. The trout were 20th-century transplants; the Incas had scooped up schools of little fish called *suche, boga,* and *carachi* in cone-shaped nets.

33

Our boat, the fastest on the lake, helped me to explore almost every cove, cliff, and rivermouth of Titicaca's hundreds of miles of shoreline, and landed me on a score of its islands. Some were uninhabited, some studded with stone temples and terraced by unknown peoples. One supported a thriving reed-boat factory; on another, the Island of the Moon, a prison stood among ruins.

The Isla del Sol—Island of the Sun—clutches Lake Titicaca like a tentacled monster. Soldier-chronicler Cieza recorded the belief that the island was the birthplace of the Inca universe: "The ancients hold...that while all was in utter darkness there rose from this island of Titicaca a resplendent sun. For this reason, they held the site to be holy, building there a temple...in honor of the sun, putting in it virgins and priests with great treasures...."

From Titicaca came the founder of the Inca dynasty, Manco Capac, and his sister-wife, Mama Ocllo, according to one prominent legend of many that the early chroniclers heard. Indeed, Bolivians today insist that the first Incas did come from the Titicaca region, and the legend is still taught in Peruvian schools. Garcilaso related it this way:

The Sun, seeing that men lived like wild animals, took pity on them and sent to earth a son and daughter; Manco Capac and Mama Ocllo would show men how to build villages and make use of the fruits of the earth. Giving them this mandate, he placed them in Lake Titicaca.

The Sun told Manco Capac and Mama Ocllo to wander where they would, and presented them with a golden staff two fingers thick. "Wherever you stop to eat or sleep, probe the earth with this golden staff," said the Sun. "Where it sinks into the soil with a single thrust...set up your court." The Sun ordained that the couple teach people to live by his wisdom and light. He promised to keep them warm, grow crops, and take a turn around the world every day to see that all went well.

The couple journeyed north until they sighted a fertile valley. Manco Capac hurled the golden staff. It sank out of sight deep into the soil. Then Manco Capac and Mama Ocllo—accompanied by many kin—wrested the valley from aboriginal tribes, according to some traditions. They built here a temple to the sun.

From such beginnings, blurred by time, rose the settlement that would become a mighty empire's capital city: Cuzco.

Garcilaso wrote that the word Cuzco signified "navel of the world" in the private tongue of the Incas. It means "richest of the rich" in the secret language of the Callawaya Indians who live in the mountains northeast of Titicaca. The multilingual Callawayas claim that this language, known only to themselves, was the native tongue the lords of Cuzco used for private conversation when they adopted Quechua as the language of the empire.

The Callawayas say that they were medicine men to the Incas. Today their descendants roam the length of the Andes peddling herbs and charms to cure fright, better the earth, and attract lovers.

Some even practice in major South American cities. Their sons attend universities but still learn herbal arts from their fathers.

I visited the land of the Callawayas with Manuel (Manolo) De Lucca, a Bolivian anthropologist who had grown up on the Island of the Sun. Manolo said, "You'll meet the headman, Octavio Magnani. That fine Italian name is a bit pretentious. He was born Mamani." The surname Mamani, one of the commonest in Bolivia, means "hawk" in Aymara, the main Titicaca tongue.

Through slashing rain, Manolo and I hiked a day beyond the end of the road to reach cloud-shrouded Curva, the mountaintop town where Octavio lived. He embraced Manolo and turned to me, shaking his head. "Ah, gringo, it will rain as long as you stay. Acomani sheds many tears whenever white men come. Always they want to steal his minerals."

"Acomani," Manolo explained, "is a mountain god, a deity peak hidden by the rain."

"But I mean to take just pictures," I protested. "Anyway, I'm only half gringo after twenty years in South America."

"I'll let Acomani know," promised Octavio.

He led us into a stone house as damp and chilly as the outdoors. An old woman crouched in a corner coughing violently.

"My wife has caught the mortal cough, like so many here," Octavio said sadly. "She is too weak to travel to a hospital."

"But you're the grand master of charms and herbs," said Manolo. "Can't you cure tuberculosis?"

The old man shrugged. *"Ah, me faltan antibióticos*—I have no antibiotics."

Yet I shouldn't question Octavio's powers, for the mountain god let up on the rain. I awoke to golden sunlight glistening from Acomani, a snow peak I judged to be nearly 20,000 feet—I have never found data for that tall but tearful god on any map.

On all sides of Curva up to 13,000 feet, the mountains were terraced for farming long ago by what surely was a far larger population than lives there now. "Somewhere near here, man first learned to cultivate potatoes," said Manolo. "The Aymara language has about 200 nouns for the potato, all sizes, colors and textures. The potato—which modern Peruvians call *papa*, as did the Incas— had much to do with the rise of Andean civilization."

Through stupendous effort, the highlanders terraced vast areas of the Andes for agriculture. Workers fitted together millions of rocks along slopes to form retaining walls, one below another. Then they filled in behind the walls with rock topped with soil. Some terraces were irrigated by gravity flow through painstakingly cut and graded stone canals.

The Incas utilized stone to the utmost: Roads, bridges, stairways, temples, palaces, storerooms, fences, aqueducts, baths, fountains, idols, tombs, tools, and weapons were of stone. Their long-range projectile was the slingstone; pebbles can be picked up everywhere, while good wood for bows does not grow in the Andes.

The lasting monuments of the Incas, their cities and fortresses, were fashioned of stone. Numerous ornamental "Inca thrones," carved in rock outcroppings, can be seen around Cuzco.

Tradition holds that Manco Capac, *(Continued on page 43)*

Clouds wrap the Bolivian village of Curva, home of Callawaya Indians whose ancestors served as medicine men to the Incas. Today's Callawayas still practice the ancient herbal arts—so successfully that few doctors or priests win acceptance near the Indians' homeland. Some healers roam South American cities, working their magic with herbs and charms to summon renewed vigor and to dispel fright. In a rural marketplace, sacks brimming with amulets—bits of aluminum, plants, and animal parts—reflect a faith in their powers older than the Inca Empire. Buyers use them to cure fever, prevent crop failure, and ensure the earth's bounty; they burn some remedies and bury or swallow others. Soothsayers provide relief when herbs and charms fail. A blind shaman (left), wearing traditional cap and cloak, listens to a supplicant asking, perhaps, for ways to recover a lost object or a wayward husband. He responds in mumbled prayer, broken by an occasional intelligible word; the listener gleans a message and leaves a coin in payment.

Rising perhaps to 20,000 feet, "God Mountain" Acomani dwarfs a llama packtrain winding through Bolivia's Apolobamba Range northeast of Lake Titicaca, a region enveloped almost

every afternoon by clouds that well up from the jungle. "Acomani sheds many tears whenever white men come," an Indian headman told the author when he arrived during a rainstorm.

Destined to serve nobility, a young girl picked for physical perfection learns cooking at a pottery stove. For four years she will study domestic skills and proper conduct at an official school for Chosen Women.

first Inca, turned into stone when he died sometime before A.D. 1300—the only Inca who was not mummified. After the conquest, to put down idolatry, the Spaniards seized mummies purported to be those of succeeding Incas. And when chroniclers inquired into Inca lineage, hundreds of Cuzco residents claimed direct descent from one or another Inca king—including Manco Capac; they also guarded traditions and relics in the memory of their ancestors. But historians have not found proof of flesh and blood in the legends of the earlier Incas.

Of Manco Capac's many children, Sinchi Roca—"War Chieftain Roca"—became second Inca. John Rowe summarizes a fable of how Sinchi Roca's mother tricked the people: "She spread the word that the sun was about to send them a ruler, and then, when all had assembled to see, brought forth her son from the mouth of a cave dressed in cloth covered with golden bangles. Dazzled by the vision, the people accepted the boy as a heaven-sent ruler."

I have seen on display in Lima's famous Mujica Gallo Museum a garment from a coastal grave which recalls Sinchi Roca's shining mantle: a tunic completely sewn with thousands of thumbnail-size plates of beaten gold.

Sinchi Roca made a small name for himself by filling Cuzco's swamps, organizing scandalous festivals, and designing the forehead fringe of red tassels which the ruling Inca wore instead of a crown. He was also the first Inca to be embalmed. His mummy, so it was claimed, was among those paraded in Cuzco for the Spaniards after they arrived some 200 years later.

The third Inca, Lloque Yupanqui—"Unforgettable Left-Handed One"—was so ugly that people fled upon seeing him. Never mind; his odd traits made him an especially holy huaca. The Incas regarded with awe, and even worshiped, everything out of the ordinary—a hunchback, twinned ears of corn, a curiously-shaped rock, the brilliant planet Venus.

When Lloque Yupanqui seemed incapable of begetting an heir, consternation swept the small kingdom. The Inca's *coya*— principal wife—became melancholy and took to drink, wrote Felipe Guamán Poma de Ayala, a 17th-century Indian artist, about his drawing of that sad queen. As the end of a lusterless reign approached without hint of heir, an oracle recommended that the old Inca try once more. A younger coya also was suggested.

The chief of a neighboring state cherished a daughter so beautiful that he thought no one good enough for her. But he changed his mind when the Son of the Sun bid for her hand.

The oracle knew best: Lloque Yupanqui begot. His son Mayta Capac became the Hercules of Inca legend. He leaped from the womb "three months after conception, robust, and with teeth, and he grew so that in one year he had the physique of eight or more, and at two years he fought with big boys and hurt them badly. All this seems fable, but I write what the natives so strongly believe ...they would kill those who contradict them." So reported

Long-necked vase portrays the dress of the Incas' Chosen Women. A mantle covers the shoulders; a tunic hangs straight from neck to ankle. Jewelry and rich embroidery at waist and at hemline signify status.

MUSEUM AND INSTITUTE OF ARCHEOLOGY, UNIVERSITY OF SAN ANTONIO ABAD, CUZCO

43

Captain Pedro Sarmiento de Gamboa, Cosmographer of the Kingdoms of Peru, appointed by the Spanish viceroy to record the oral history of the Incas.

Sarmiento's history, including information gathered on a viceregal tour of the realm, stands alone. He read the text in Cuzco to 42 Indians of various factions, some old enough to have been schooled in Inca tradition before the Spaniards came. Their corrections were incorporated in the copy sent to King Philip in 1572.

Sarmiento wrote that "at a very tender age" Mayta Capac killed some Cuzco aborigines, the valley's pre-Inca people, provoking an uprising which the Inca lords barely managed to quell. As a result, said other chroniclers, the child prodigy was hastily given the customary maturity ceremony. The rite involved llama sacrifices, flagellation, a footrace, and the bestowal of a sling, shield, mace, and finally the piercing of his ears. And he was awarded his adult name and his *wara*—breechclout.

High Inca nobles were distinguished by their short haircuts and huge earplugs: "He who had the largest [ears] was held to be the finest gentleman . . ." noted Pizarro's cousin, astonished to see Inca earlobes that touched the shoulder. Another Spaniard observed that some ear disks were as wide as a large orange.

Despite his reputation for belligerence, Mayta Capac made no attempt to push the Inca state beyond Cuzco—a valley so narrow I have walked across it from the eastern hilltops to the western in four hours. Although chiefs from faraway nations did visit him in Cuzco, Mayta Capac's preoccupation, according to one story, was the study of wizardry. At his death, the council of nobles elected his son Capac Yupanqui to be fifth Inca, following the Inca custom of naming the most capable son, not necessarily the firstborn, as heir.

With Capac Yupanqui—"Unforgettable King"—Inca history begins emerging from legend. Some chroniclers say that he was the first Inca to engage in battle and exact tribute from tribes beyond the hitherto insignificant valley of Cuzco. A sortie of a day or two in any direction from Cuzco took Capac Yupanqui's marauders into territory of tribes who spoke different languages. Some 200 miles southeast, two states controlled by the Colla and Lupaca tribes held the Titicaca shores. Almost as far to the west, the belligerent Chancas threatened neighboring tribes.

The Chancas lived near the heart of a long-forgotten civilization to which archeologists have given the name Huari. From A.D. 600 to 800, the influence of the Huari culture—some say empire—spread from the central highlands to nearly all of Peru. Huari technology and urban planning left a stamp on the Peruvian Andes. One Huari provincial center and stores depot—Piquillacta, or Flea Town—stands beside the highway to Titicaca 30 minutes' drive from Cuzco. The fieldstone ruins fill about a square kilometer.

When Capac Yupanqui died and was mummified, emissaries came from afar. They attended his funeral rites and the enthronement of his heir, Inca Roca, sixth of the dynasty and the first ruler to add to his name "Inca," a term of nobility.

Inca Roca conducted the affairs of state from a throne better described as a royal stool, a concave seat about eight inches high carved of red wood and covered with fine cloth. A taller chair would

Ears of corn, a staple in the highland diet, dry in the yard of a Peruvian farmer. When ground, boiled, and fermented, corn produces chicha—a potent beverage. Incas used foot plows to break the earth on rugged, narrow slopes. Before planting, a farmer cuts the soil while his wife turns over hard-packed clods.

Farming tools and methods from Inca times continue in Bolivia, where a Chipaya Indian mother winnows quinua—once sustenance for Inca armies. Quinua, with its hard-shelled seeds (above), thrives at elevations ranging from two miles up to the snowline—the zone where most Andean people dwell. Highland women (right) fertilize a field of potatoes. Inca farmers produced far more food than the empire needed. The people consumed one part and stored a portion against famine; priests burned the rest as offerings to the gods.

have been as impractical for him as for commoners since Andean man used no table; then, as today, he ate from a cloth or mat spread on the ground.

The three main staples in Inca meals, or in any soldier's knotted bundle of rations, for that matter, were drawn from public granaries: *sara*—corn, *chuño*—dehydrated potato, and *quinua*—a relative of the pigweed. In the Andes, where climate varies from polar to equatorial in four vertical miles, these dried foods came from different elevations. Surpluses were stored for use in time of famine or war, when the soldier-farmer had to abandon his land.

Quinua, a heavily-seeded stalk, grows well above timberline, tolerating frost and drought and turning every color of autumn leaves as it ripens. Indians uproot the plant, thresh it by clubbing, winnow the spherical seeds, and use them as cereal for making flour and thickening soups.

Since ancient times, Indians have produced dehydrated potatoes in June, when the Andean day is warm and cloudless and night temperatures fall below freezing at 12,000 feet. Small potatoes are spread on the ground to freeze overnight and to thaw in the sunny morning. After gathering them into little piles before noon, men and women tread on them with bare feet. Water squirts out of the potatoes because freezing has ruptured the cells. Then they are spread again to dry, becoming chuño; it will keep for months—or almost indefinitely if ground into meal.

"It turns back into potato, even better, when reconstituted with water," insists my son Lance, who grew up on chuño. Personally, I can't stomach the stuff except in meaty soups.

Corn, which thrives at lower altitudes than potatoes or quinua, was highly esteemed for religious ceremonies and for making *chicha*, a cloudy beer. Chicha was consumed in enormous quantities to produce ritual intoxication. It remains the principal highland beverage.

As commerce with other tribes increased, the diet of the Incas expanded to include still other staples unknown in the Old World: squash, sweet potatoes, manioc, peanuts, and fruits such as pineapple, papaya, and avocado. Since the Inca lived in Cuzco, silver from veins in the earth and gold from alluvial deposits were also brought from afar.

Garcilaso wrote that Inca Roca founded a four-year school for boys of high birth. They studied Quechua, religion, quipus, and history. He also associated Inca Roca with an institution that "Spanish historians skipped over like a cat on hot embers": the Chosen Women, some of whom the Inca picked for his seraglio.

In Cuzco, girls eight and under were selected as "Brides of the Sun" according to beauty and untainted lineage. They lived as novices in convents supervised by *mamacuna*, celibate matrons who taught spinning, weaving, sewing royal garments, and making holy bread. Many remained all their lives in their quarters, which were inviolate. A nun who failed to keep her vow was buried alive and her accomplice hanged with all his relatives, wrote Garcilaso. His town was torn down and strewn with stones. But a nun was not punished, added another chronicler, if she claimed the Sun had fathered her child.

Student at the school for boys in Cuzco watches intently as an amauta, or wise man, instructs him in recording data on a quipu. Sons of nobility devoted four years to the formal study of the language, religion, and history of the Incas.

49

Inca Roca began his reign as a disciplinarian and ended a voluptuary. At his death, "many of the women who had loved and served him during his life ... hanged themselves by their own hair ..." reported Cieza.

As a boy the seventh Inca, Yahuar Huacac—"He Who Weeps Blood"—was kidnaped by neighboring tribesmen. They threatened to kill him; he wept tears of blood and was spared because this oddity made him awesome, according to several chroniclers.

It seemed likelier to other chroniclers, and to me, that he simply suffered from a bad case of bloodshot eyes. Many mountain folk are red-eyed from drink and smoke: not tobacco smoke—the Incas didn't burn tobacco, nor do many highland Indians today— but cooking-fire smoke. Most Indian huts are windowless single rooms of sod, adobe, or stone, thatched with yellow bunchgrass and lacking chimneys. At daybreak and dusk, every village in the highlands, and every isolated peasant's hut, appears to be on fire as mealtime smoke filters through the thatch.

On a week's walk over the mountains to the jungle east of Cuzco I once took shelter in such a hut just below a 15,000-foot pass. Going inside, I banged my head on the stone lintel of a doorway less than four feet high.

The widowed owner, Catalina Apasa, motioned me to a dark corner. Her grown sons, both llama herders, drew a hide over the doorway to keep out wind and dogs. A rooster lived inside, as did guinea pigs, which have shared Andean man's abode for thousands of years, ending up in his cookpot.

To bring potatoes to a boil, Catalina blew on a dung-and-twig fire with a tube, adding soot to the smoke in my eyes. I covered my corner of the dirt floor with a poncho and sleeping bag. One of the herders yanked a couple of filthy iron-hard llama pelts from the rafters—"For your bed," he said—thoroughly dirtying my layout. The dirt didn't wiggle; few vermin exist at that altitude. Catalina handed me a heaping bowl containing 30 to 40 tiny unpeeled potatoes—far more than I could possibly eat. I stood, cracking my head against a frozen llama shank that hung from the ceiling. I berated the shank in English. Catalina—who spoke only Quechua—took this to mean that I wanted llama meat and roasted a piece for me.

Soon, huddled in hides, the family dozed off sitting against the walls. I put my toilet articles on a massive flat rock beside my head and curled up in my sleeping bag. Guinea pigs scampered across me, one over my face. Catalina, awakened by my exclamation, threw a handful of greens into an opposite corner. The guinea pigs went there to dine.

Sleeping fitfully, I gasped for oxygen every few minutes. It was still dark when I felt a small weight placed on top of my sleeping bag, then another and another. Crunching and clunking sounds followed. I flicked on my flashlight. In utter darkness a man had piled my belongings on my chest and was rocking a big half-moon-shaped stone back and forth on my "bedside table." He was grinding quinua. Catalina, with a potato breakfast in mind, blew the embers into flame. The cock roosting over my head thought it was daylight and crowed mightily.

Awakening to the sun's first rays, llamas and alpacas stir near the buildings of a family farm in the mountains of southeastern Peru. Inside one of the thatched stone huts, Catalina Apasa—up long before daybreak—brings potatoes to a boil. She and her herder sons —much like the Incas before them —rely on llamas as pack animals and as a source of food and wool; they also collect droppings for fuel and fertilizer. Some high-landers still cling to the Inca tra-dition of burying a llama fetus under their houses to propiti-ate gods and to bring good fortune.

I sat up, my head entering a wreath of suffocating smoke. I slipped outside and shivered in cold fresh air until dawn. One of the sons came out to keep me company and began to play a *quena,* an Inca-style flute with a pentatonic scale.

While he tootled mournful tunes, yellow sunlight stole down the mountainside, and I saw that we were surrounded by scores of silent llamas and alpacas of many colors and markings. They opened their large eyes but remained sitting like woolen shrubs, their legs folded under them camel-fashion. The llama herder readied the animals' packs of homespun woolen sacks filled with potatoes. After the sun's rays warmed them, the llamas jackknifed to their feet and soon grouped to receive their loads.

In the Cuzco-Titicaca region, man has long been so dependent on llamas, and they on him, that the relationship is truly symbiotic; there are no wild llama populations. For Catalina, as for the Incas, a llama is a source of wool and some companionship, as well as a beast of burden and a producer of fuel and fertilizer. After its death, a llama provides a hide and good-tasting meat which can be sun dried and preserved as *charqui*—a Quechua word and the source of our term "jerky."

Catalina's sons and other men of this region are among the few people in the Andes who still wear the Inca-style tunic, a sleeveless, thigh-length pullover shirt. However, their forebears remained outside Inca influence until after the reign of the eighth Inca.

As a prince, that future ruler claimed to have seen Viracocha—the lord creator—in a dream. Upon becoming Inca, he presumptuously took the name of Viracocha for his own. Considering himself predestined for greatness, Viracocha Inca set out to conquer everyone around Cuzco. He liquidated chieftains, destroyed rebellious towns, and formed alliances with the Lupacas, who lived near Lake Titicaca, and with the Quechua nation on the west bank of the Apurimac gorge. His fame spread.

But the powerful Chancas, who lived two weeks' march west of Cuzco, considered the Incas mere upstarts who absurdly pretended that the sun was their father. The Chancas believed themselves to be descended from the puma, and wore feline heads on top of their own, wrote Garcilaso. They plaited their long hair in many tiny braids, and used fierce war paint made of vermilion from the mercury mines at Huancavelica.

For years the Chanca chieftains—one called himself Lord of All the Earth—edged ever closer to the Inca capital, swallowing up the Quechua nation en route. Finally, a Chanca general demanded Cuzco's capitulation, lest he dye his lance in Inca blood.

Viracocha, now old and enfeebled, abandoned Cuzco. He withdrew to a fortified country estate, accompanied by his women and a weak, sybaritic son, Urcon, whom he had chosen as his successor. It was about A.D. 1438. Two centuries' rule of Cuzco by the Inca dynasty seemed fated to end that year.

But many a great civilization has flowered in response to a mortal challenge. Standing fast in Cuzco was another son of Viracocha, one who would be, in the view of two eminent historians, "the greatest man that the aboriginal race of America has produced": Inca Yupanqui. He would become the mighty Pachacuti.

Footwork brings respite from fieldwork as boys romp with a yarn ball in Queros, an isolated mountain enclave of Inca tradition near Cuzco. Trails so steep that even llamas sometimes stumble lead to terraced fields that lie a day's climb from the community of some 40 families. Large stone houses hold the villagers' harvest of corn and potatoes.

Lord Inca

On a ridge above sun-washed Cuzco, a woman weaves a poncho using a traditional backstrap loom. From these heights about 1438, a young prince led Inca slingmen to victory over a powerful force of Chanca warriors attacking the town. He became Pachacuti, first emperor, and during the next 25 years expanded the Inca domain outward from Cuzco.

Cataclysm

GOLD ALPACA FOUND AT THE TEMPLE OF THE SUN. ACTUAL SIZE. MUSEUM AND INSTITUTE OF ARCHEOLOGY, UNIVERSITY OF SAN ANTONIO ABAD, CUZCO

THEY WITNESSED the birth of an empire, those spectators who gathered on the heights above Cuzco one day around A.D. 1438. A young prince, Inca Yupanqui—he had not yet earned the name Pachacuti—had summoned warriors to defend the Inca capital from the Chanca army. But most of the recruits chose not to commit themselves and withdrew to the hills to watch the battle.

Combat was joined with boasting and defiant shouts meant to intimidate the foe. Inca slingmen drew first blood, for their stones outranged Chanca lances. Most Indian fighting was free-for-all and hand-to-hand, but Prince Inca Yupanqui and his generals hewed straight for the sacred idol that the Chancas carried.

The Incas captured the idol, striking terror into Chanca hearts. Some panicked. As soon as spectators saw that the tide of battle was turning in favor of the Incas, they poured from the hills and helped pursue the fleeing Chancas, stripping the wounded and dead of weapons and ornaments and turning the retreat into a rout.

After the victory, Inca Yupanqui spread word of a miracle: The Incas had won, he said, because "even the rocks turned to warriors" fighting on his side. From then on, Inca armies enjoyed a fearful reputation for divine intervention. They bore into battle platforms of sacred stones named for immortal warriors. In years to come, many Inca enemies gave up without a fight rather than risk being felled by invisible bowmen whom the stones represented.

A popular rhyme grimly depicted the fate of those who dared oppose Inca might:

> We'll drink chicha from your skull
> From your teeth we'll make a necklace
> From your bones, flutes
> From your skin we'll make a drum
> And then we'll dance.

Cuzco's victorious warriors stuffed the skins of the Chanca chieftains with ashes and straw. At the battle site the Incas built a large mausoleum for the dummies, and seated some of them with

elbows bent. When the wind blew, arms fluttered and mummified fingers beat a macabre tattoo on the drumhead-taut bellies. It was a formidable reminder of the event that launched the Incas on their trajectory of empire.

"The hall of the defeated dead with its pitiful drums stood by the western approaches to Cuzco for every passerby to see, including Spaniards who came that way a century later," said a Cuzco friend, Dr. Luis A. Pardo. Director Emeritus of the Museum and Institute of Archeology, University of San Antonio Abad, in Cuzco, he lives in a house whose front wall—like many others in town—was built of stone by the Incas. Don Luis accompanied Sue and me one day to a hillside overlooking Cuzco. He described how it probably appeared at the time of the Chanca attack.

"It was more a compound inhabited by nobles and their retinues than a town as we think of it," he said. "Most walls were sod or adobe—finely wrought stone came later. Roofs were thatched with yellow bunchgrass. The Huatanay River, which rises just above the town, was channeled in stonework even then. I remember watching laborers remove ancient solid stone bridges and build the present Avenida del Sol over the river. Today, at the upper end of town, the Huatanay is still a crystalline spring; at the lower end, a sewer.

"The Plaza de Armas down there," continued don Luis, pointing to the only open block in the city center, "was the great square, Haucaypata, of Inca times; it hasn't changed much. Since Cuzco was the religious center of the realm, ceremonies and sacrifices were held there most days of the year. On the day of the battle the plaza must have seemed strangely empty of celebrants and llamas. That day the hillside farmers put away their *chaqui tacllas*—foot plows—and took up slings and clubs and shields to stop the Chancas. They made Andean history."

The reigning Inca, Viracocha, had conceded victory to the Chancas and left Cuzco. Now he was displeased by Inca Yupanqui's success, for he wanted another son, Prince Urcon, to become Inca. He refused to return to Cuzco from self-imposed exile.

The lords of Cuzco awarded the red-tassled forehead fringe of office to the bold and steadfast Inca Yupanqui. Thus, the young defender of Cuzco's gates suddenly became a conquering warlord holding sway over a stretch of rugged and varied highlands between the Vilcanota and Apurimac rivers, an area somewhat less than that of Lake Titicaca, 3,200 square miles.

As if anticipating the transcendental role that destiny held in store, he named himself Pachacuti—Quechua for "cataclysm." Pachacuti is formed of the noun *pacha*—earth, universe, world-time—and the verb *kutiy*—return, restore, overturn. Some chroniclers translated the name as "he who transforms the earth."

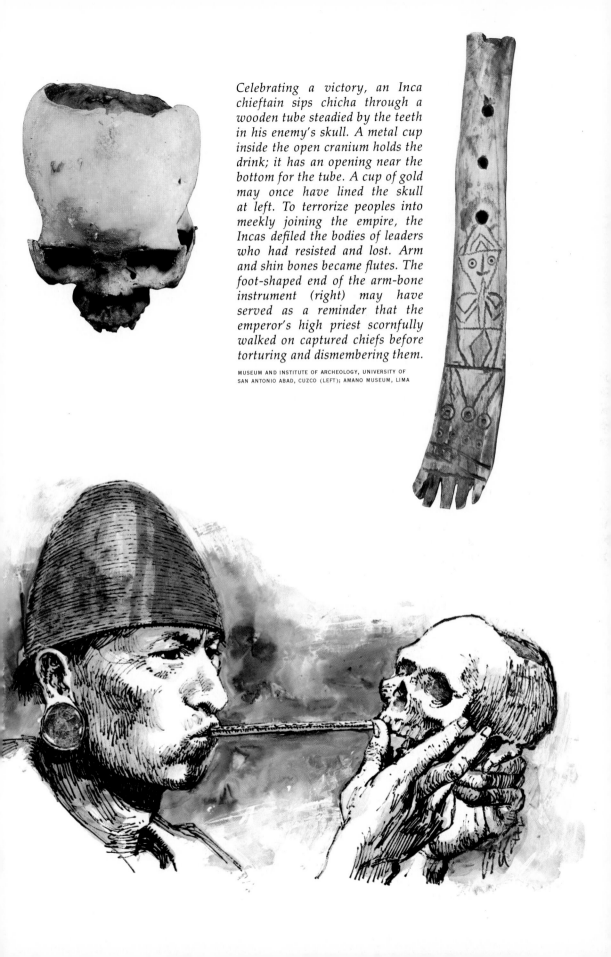

Celebrating a victory, an Inca chieftain sips chicha through a wooden tube steadied by the teeth in his enemy's skull. A metal cup inside the open cranium holds the drink; it has an opening near the bottom for the tube. A cup of gold may once have lined the skull at left. To terrorize peoples into meekly joining the empire, the Incas defiled the bodies of leaders who had resisted and lost. Arm and shin bones became flutes. The foot-shaped end of the arm-bone instrument (right) may have served as a reminder that the emperor's high priest scornfully walked on captured chiefs before torturing and dismembering them.

MUSEUM AND INSTITUTE OF ARCHEOLOGY, UNIVERSITY OF
SAN ANTONIO ABAD, CUZCO (LEFT); AMANO MUSEUM, LIMA

Pachacuti lived up to either version. The ninth Inca ruler widened his power to become first Inca emperor. So thoroughly did he alter his Andean world that it has never since been the same.

Succession of the Incas often was marked with dissension. Power shifts produced savage resentment. Tradition hints that Pachacuti's father or brother ambushed him, but his guards cut down the would-be assassins. In retaliation, Pachacuti pruned Prince Urcon from the official list of the Inca dynasty, so that historians never really knew what happened to the weakling. The soldier-chronicler Cieza says that when he asked old men about Urcon's fate, they just laughed.

Early in his reign, Pachacuti resolved to rebuild Cuzco as a monument to Inca glory and as a ceremonial center to impress pilgrims from afar. If the emperor's ghost looks down on Cuzco from some Olympus reserved for rulers who have left an indelible stamp on human affairs, surely that royal shade would not be altogether displeased with the way his plan has turned out.

His artisans worked in stone. Consequently, many of their spectacular creations have survived nearly five centuries of earthquake, war, and wrenching urban alteration which began in the 16th century with the arrival of the Spaniards.

Every year tens of thousands of visitors see the ruins. A lifelong friend, Admiral Alberto Jimenez de Lucio, told me that buildings begun by Pachacuti accounted for much of the 45 million tourist dollars that Cuzco received last year. Alberto, a graduate of the United States Naval Academy and Massachusetts Institute of Technology, is Peru's Minister of Industry and Tourism.

With Alberto's wife, Zoila, Sue and I once roamed Cuzco for days, finding dozens of hidden walls and many streets where precisely fitted stone foundations still stand at the passerby's elbow. Pachacuti designed his city in the shape of a puma, evoking the feline cult common to many Andean cultures. Streets and avenues crisscross in slightly trapezoidal patterns. Doors, windows, and niches also are trapezoids—narrowing at the top—a feature that makes late Inca architecture instantly recognizable.

"But how," wondered Zoila, "did they cut those polygonal stones—such strange shapes—and fit them together so well?"

Dr. Manuel Chávez Ballón, a resident archeologist, gave us the answer. The Inca stonemasons worked from models of clay and sometimes stone. They split rock by drilling small holes and then wedging it apart. Their main tools were of stone—hammers and axes—although they also used bronze chisels, and they laboriously polished rock with sand and water.

With a map constructed by Dr. Chávez, it was easy to follow main highways from the north, south, east, and west as they converged on Haucaypata, once the plaza of the idols and now the central square of modern Cuzco. Few bits of earth have been so saturated with exultation, tragedy, and blood as Haucaypata. Idols and mummies of kings were paraded there and worshiped. At least 100 llamas a month were sacrificed in routine festivals. And at special, solemn ceremonies for deliverance from pestilence, drought, or reverses in warfare, offerings even included the sacrificing of unblemished children.

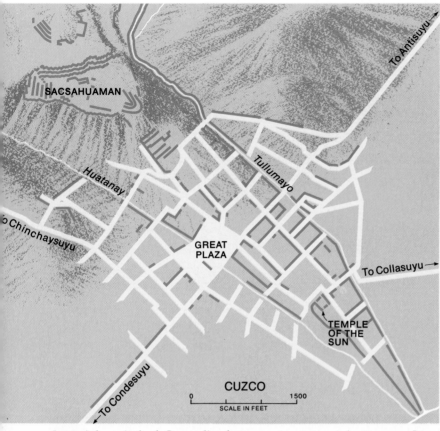

Imperial capital of Cuzco lies between two mountain streams. Incas built the city roughly in the shape of a puma — a feline divinity — with Sacsahuaman as the head. Red lines indicate Inca walls still intact.

To an April festival honoring royalty came Napa, the white llama, wearing a red shirt and golden ear ornaments. Napa took part in frequent ceremonies, chewed coca, drank chicha, and was never sacrificed. The royal llama offered chicha to the gods by kicking over crocks of the beverage.

With visions of such ceremonies filling my mind, I daydreamed one Sunday morning on a bench in that historic square. An off-key fanfare of trumpets roused me, and I watched a religious procession turn the corner. La Virgen de Belén was making her annual peregrination to various churches in the city, attended — it seemed to me — by a measure of melancholy and a note of nostalgia. Ornate in her silks and golden crown, the Virgin stood high on a massive platform borne by 12 Indians, their normally impassive faces contorted by effort and ecstasy. A priest and a youngster bearing a church banner escorted her, along with two altar boys swinging silver pots of smoking incense on silver chains.

When the scent touched my nostrils I recalled Indian offerings of burnt coca leaves. It was easy to imagine prisoners of war parading huge bales of the leaf and baskets of decorative jungle-bird feathers through Haucaypata square, as they must have done when Pachacuti's armies returned from a jungle campaign. Cieza tells how they advanced into the Amazon watershed, the steeply sloping

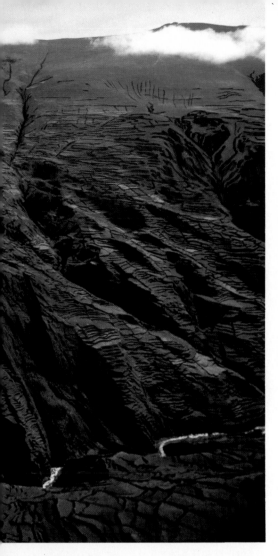

Step by step, terraced farms climb to the top of a 13,000-foot-high slope (above left) northeast of Lake Titicaca. Callawaya Indians grow potatoes on these earthen strips. Highland farmers began cultivating potatoes in the Andes in ancient times. Corn, the sacred grain of the Incas, thrives at lower elevations; the curving terraces (left) at Pisac, near Cuzco, rise to about 11,000 feet. At ceremonial centers lying in ruins atop the terraces at far left, Incas burned corn as offerings to the gods. Rock walls 15 feet high (above) level the earth for agriculture and hold it against erosion caused by violent summer rainstorms. Stones jutting from the walls serve as steps between terraces. Emperor Pachacuti's engineers designed these irrigated plots; workers, paying their taxes in labor, built them during the 15th century. On terraces such as these, the Incas produced food for their expanding empire.

Struck by a nine-inch blowgun dart, a cock-of-the-rock falls to a jungle hunter. The plumage of such brightly-colored birds, taken to Cuzco, decorated the ceremonial tunics and headdresses of many Inca nobles.

jungle that became part of Antisuyu, the empire's eastern quarter. Cieza called this region "las montañas de los Andes," and Peruvians still refer to that jungle as "la montaña." From the root of Antisuyu came "Andes," name of the world's longest and second highest mountain system.

Viewing the Virgin's procession through drowsy eyes, I conjured a tableau of excited citizens reviling naked and shivering prisoners whose red paint ran awry down their noses — noses soft and short compared with the haughty beaks of the highlanders. Inca guards brandished maces and stubby shields, happy to have returned alive from the jungle, where their tunics had rotted in the warm rain and were riddled by voracious ants and enemy arrows.

Down in that dark world of insects, disease, and poison-tipped blowgun darts, the highlanders would have found no open fields for proper battles, only gigantic green labyrinths without horizon. Shadowed even at noon by the leafy forest crown, the undergrowth was threaded by barely perceptible trails. In my mind, I could picture warriors in single file squeezing through by lifting feet high and bending heads low, watching all the while for little venomous snakes, large constrictors, and unclad bowmen.

The savages—ignorant of Pachacuti's reputation for receiving divine aid—doubtless sent six-foot arrows flitting among the trees and thunking into the invaders who had removed padded cotton armor seeking relief from oppressive heat. Survivors complained to Pachacuti of monstrous snakes. He sent a second expedition with a sorceress to render the reptiles harmless. In any event, the Incas won this time by battle and blandishments.

On another campaign Pachacuti advanced into the Chinchaysuyu, the populous northwest quarter of the Inca world. He marched about 200 miles, beyond the Chanca homeland, extending the empire and spreading the gospel of the Sun.

At this time, other highland chieftains also were subjugating their neighbors. Chuchi Capac, a warlord of the Lake Titicaca basin, had even usurped the title "Inca." Chuchi Capac had seized about 500 miles of altiplano ranging from Titicaca's fertile shores

Completing his morning makeup, a jungle chief—wearing macaw-feather ear ornaments and necklaces of glass, shell, and boar's teeth—draws a red line near his blackened lips. Many peoples on the eastern flank of the

Andes continue the ancient custom of painting their faces with designs—like that on the foot-high Inca-style wooden cup above. Pulpy achiote seeds inside a freshly cut pod yield reddish pigment when mashed into paste.

to the rainless deserts of northern Chile. Pachacuti sent emissaries demanding Chuchi Capac's capitulation; the warlord replied that he would be delighted to accept Pachacuti's homage, or if he preferred to fight, to make a goblet from his skull.

The Inca state was well-prepared for such wars. Great bins overflowed with dried and dehydrated food: corn, quinua, charqui, and chuño. Woolens, weapons, cordage, and sandals filled warehouses. Vassals in the provinces busily constructed hard-surface roads by order of their Inca governors. Herders rounded up llamas by the thousand to bear the paraphernalia of war; the llamas would live off the countryside during campaigns, slowing now and then to nibble clumps of *ichu,* a bunchgrass. They carried 80 pounds or so, less than Andean man's limit.

Pachacuti could call on vast reserves of manpower. During the short sowing and reaping seasons, farmers grew foodstuffs far in excess of demand. When they were at war, neighbors tended their fields. In this land without money, the main tax was a period of forced labor, the *mita,* Quechua for "a turn." Quipu camayocs — accountants — consulted their knotted strings to determine how many could be spared from agriculture to take a turn at public works, mining, or military service.

Forced labor kept subjects out of mischief, but they had ample leisure for festivities and ritual drinking: Commoners enjoyed a large number of holidays. But they could not enjoy ordinary idleness; the Incas invented work to keep them busy. Crimes were considered disobedience to the Inca. Punishments included public rebuke, exile to the coca plantations, torture, and the *hiwaya:* dropping a big rock on a man's back. Death penalties, imposed after trial by the Inca or a governor with all witnesses present, consisted of stoning, hanging by the feet, throwing from a cliff, or beating in the head with a club. Strict law enforcement and lack of want made crime extremely rare.

Rigid Inca rule combined with success in war strengthened morale. The people possessed self-confidence. Under Pachacuti's inspired leadership, the citizen armies now marched on the Collasuyu, the western highlands of present-day Bolivia, accepting the challenge of Chuchi Capac, the self-styled Inca. En route, Pachacuti destroyed a rebellious district and doubtless impressed fresh recruits from subservient peoples. On the Titicaca shore he assumed command and plunged into battle. Quickly defeating the Colla nation, he captured Chuchi Capac, and seized valuable booty.

Celebration followed Pachacuti's triumphant return to Cuzco. Enemy huacas — sacred objects — were displayed and the Inca's priest trod symbolically upon the spoils and prisoners. Pachacuti had Chuchi Capac beheaded in the great square, and committed lesser captains to a dungeon full of serpents and toads. The Inca's prestige grew so great that subjects entered his presence barefoot, with downcast eyes, and bearing token burdens on their backs.

Chroniclers also reported that Pachacuti overran the region

Red-tasseled fringe — insignia of the Inca ruler — crowns Pachacuti in this portrait modeled after a native of Cuzco of today. Eminent historians consider Pachacuti the greatest of American Indians.

Shadowy light of Mama Kilya, Mother Moon, spreads over a Chipaya Indian village in southwestern Bolivia. Round sod houses resemble those found elsewhere in the lands of the Inca Empire. Long grasses thatch their roofs, and cactus-wood doors close their single entrances, which always face east. The Incas used wood for many household utensils; a foot-high, Inca-style cup — or kero — takes the shape of a puma's head.

between Cuzco and the sea, called Condesuyu. If so, he had then forayed into all quarters of the Tahuantinsuyu: northeast to Antisuyu's jungled mountains; southeast to Collasuyu's Titicaca and beyond; southwest to Condesuyu's bleak highlands and coast; and northwest to Chinchaysuyu's mountain valleys and desert oases.

The Inca decreed that farmland be used for three purposes: to be cultivated for religion, providing vast quantities of food and textiles to be burned as offerings; to support government and fill warehouses for distribution in war or famine; and to provide just enough food for the populace. Quipu camayocs regulated the business of this womb-to-tomb society.

Pachacuti's religious fervor also transformed the imperial capital. He emptied Cuzco of inhabitants to rebuild it as a holy place, lavishing booty on the spiritual center of the realm: Coricancha, the "golden enclosure." Magnificent stone walls, one a sweeping parabola, enclosed a complex of temples hung with tapestries and housing images of Inca deities. Commoners were denied entrance. Chosen Women maintained a sacred flame. They burned so much firewood that the countryside around Cuzco was denuded of trees; they offered huge amounts of food and fine clothing to the gods, especially the Sun.

Inti, the Sun, divine ancestor of the Inca dynasty, ranked first among several sky gods that served the creator Viracocha. The gold-arrayed Sun Temple stood as the finest in the land. It sheltered not only the Sun image—a golden disk embossed with a human face—but also an effigy, Punchao, a solid gold Sun-child. A chalice lodged in Punchao's body contained dust of the hearts of bygone Inca rulers.

The Sun's consort was Mama Kilya, Mother Moon. Her image inhabited an adjacent chapel adorned with silver. She marked the time of festivals. On Lake Titicaca I once watched the shadow of an eclipse stealing across the moon's face. "A puma is trying to eat her," a Bolivian fisherman explained to me solemnly as he exploded firecrackers to scare the puma away. Centuries before him, the highlanders had shouted, whipped dogs to make them howl, blown trumpets, beaten drums, shot arrows toward the moon, and brandished lances, as if to wound a snake or mountain lion and prevent it from devouring the moon or tearing it to pieces.

Another sky deity was Ilyapa, the Thunder, God of Weather. A constellation, to the Incas he took the form of a warrior armed with a sling. When Ilyapa cast his lightning bolt, he made a clap of thunder—as when a slingstone is hurled smartly, causing the free end of the sling to crack like a whip. Ilyapa's sister, as a lovely Quechua poem tells, drew rainwater from a heavenly river, the Milky Way, and kept it in a jug. When Ilyapa's thunderbolt broke his sister's jug, rain fell upon the earth.

Within the walls of Coricancha, Incas glorified these gods with a resplendent display of gold: slabs of gold on temple walls, delicate golden fountains and massive golden altars, a garden full of goldsmiths' notions of corn and lizards and hummingbirds, life-size golden llamas, masks of gold worn by old women who fanned flies from gold-bedecked mummies of kings.

Such treasures the Spaniards looted from the Temple of the

Sun in the early days of conquest. But they did not raze the building. Later Dominican friars erected their own great temple on top of Coricancha. Not only would the Indians continue to worship at the same place, but some of the old temple's cut building stone also could be used for the Catholic church. For four centuries all that remained to be seen of the spiritual heart of Pachacuti's empire were hundreds of yards of magnificent coursed masonry, 15-foot outer walls stripped of their golden friezes, the parabolic retaining wall, and a few monastic cells with trapezoidal doorways inside Santo Domingo church.

In May 1950 an earthquake smote Cuzco and demolished the church. It struck a single sledgehammer blow, quite unlike the typical minutes-long upheaval followed by days and weeks of wrenching aftershocks. These long convulsions shake stupendous landslides from Andean heights and clog river valleys when Pacha Kuyuchik, God of Earthquakes, tosses in his sleep.

I entered Cuzco not long after that instant clap of doomsday in 1950, picking my way among stone blocks flung from Inca walls like big black dice onto the cobbled streets. Surely this had been the sharpest quake since Pachacuti's day. Colonial buildings leaned and lurched; their second-story bedrooms—with front walls destroyed—were open to the streets and public squares as if they were theatrical sets. The Dominican church had caved in. "Not the first time, but the worst," a priest ruefully remarked.

After tons of shattered masonry were cleared and layers of paint and plaster were scraped away to start the restoration of Santo Domingo, a wonderful thing emerged from all that havoc. Beneath the church several original Coricancha structures were found intact, their splendid walls undamaged by time or earthquake. Some of the finest Inca stonework had been protected by the act of building Santo Domingo church on top of it.

Coricancha restoration proceeds, though it is hindered by lack of funds and by the mass of the reconstructed Catholic church. The resident Dominicans have moved out of their cells—the Inca shrines they occupied for four centuries—and opened them to tourists. Dr. Luis Barreda Murillo, an archeologist at the university in Cuzco, dug up a five-inch gold statuette in the church patio that somehow was overlooked amid all the looting. "We were fortunate to find this relic of one of the world's richest treasuries of goldsmiths' art," he told me.

The Cuzco buildings where Pachacuti stored clay terrain models, and possibly quipu records of conquered territories, must have been a busy place in the 1450's. With perhaps a million citizens to keep occupied, and with a crusader's drive to impress the Inca religion and way of life on all mankind, Pachacuti beat harder on the drum of conquest. But increasingly he ran the affairs of empire and laid down laws from Cuzco while his generals—nearly all kinsmen—took to the field.

Pachacuti lent his own golden weapons to his brother Capac Yupanqui for a limited thrust with 70,000 men into the populous Chinchaysuyu, northwest of Cuzco. Emissaries had prepared the way so well that Capac Yupanqui at first met little resistance. Even the Chancas, once deadly enemies, joined his army and

Outer wall of the Incas' Coricancha—"golden enclosure"—of the Temple of the Sun in Cuzco curves around the Catholic church and convent of Santo Domingo, founded in 1534. Within the temple grounds (below), the author's wife, Sue, measures a hewn stone in an alcove of a chapel; two Indians pause near the Santa Catalina nunnery wall that once guarded the palace of the Chosen Women. In Inca times, no one entered except on sacred occasions.

fought so well they outshone the Incas. Then, fearing Inca treachery, the entire Chanca contingent—men, women, and children—fled north into Amazon headwater forest beyond Chachapoyas.

In vain, Capac Yupanqui pursued them hundreds of mountain miles beyond the limits of conquest set by Pachacuti. Then he turned to crush Cajamarca, highland ally of the formidable Kingdom of Chimor which ruled the north coast of Peru. The capture of Cajamarca, a name to be forever linked with the collapse of the Inca Empire, signaled Capac Yupanqui's downfall. At the victory celebration he boasted that he had gained more land than his brother, the Inca. Pachacuti ordered Capac Yupanqui home, then had him beheaded just before he arrived.

Why? He had forayed too far; he had let the Chancas escape. Too, the return of a triumphant hero with his army would have endangered Pachacuti, who wished, anyway, that the honor of far-flung conquest had fallen to his favorite son, Tupa Inca Yupanqui. Thenceforth, Tupa Inca spearheaded major campaigns, becoming one of the most formidable and far-ranging conquerors of all time.

Pachacuti spent the rest of a long life perfecting the art of imperial management. He shifted populations and stirred them into the royal mixing bowl to unify speech and customs. To establish the census and assess taxes, the Inca divided lifetimes into 12 stages, from infancy to old age. He also enforced laws that regulated travel, dress, marriage, worship, and proper behavior. And he continued building Sacsahuaman, the fortress which still commands the steep rise overlooking Cuzco from the north.

"He ordered twenty thousand men sent in from the provinces," reported Cieza. "Four thousand to quarry and cut; six thousand to haul..." and the rest to shape the stone and to erect walls and towers. Garcilaso described the fortress as a witness to the majesty of the Incas and of incredible proportions, so extraordinary that it seemed as if magic presided over its construction, a greater work than the seven wonders of the world, and more like pieces of mountain than mere building stones.

So gigantic is the fortress that later observers perpetuated a myth that only supernaturals could have built it. To Spaniards in colonial times, most Indians appeared to be downtrodden and devoid of creativity. Chroniclers were unwilling to credit Pachacuti and his craftsmen with engineering genius and astonishing skill at shaping stone.

One wrote that Sacsahuaman was assembled by black arts; two said the Devil built it. Three thought it was the work of giants, and three believed the Incas knew how to melt rocks. Two said certain ancient waters turned wood into stone. By the 19th century two writers suspected the Incas knew an herb for softening and shaping rocks.

Extraterrestrials got into the act in the 20th century. Nowadays, drugstore paperbacks speculate that Sacsahuaman was built by creatures from outer space. At the great Inti Raymi sun pageant, held at Sacsahuaman every 24th of June, an official once earnestly informed Sue that Martians had constructed the fortress. "Not the little green men, of course. But *big* green men."

Pachacuti would be amused.

Under lowering skies, herders trail llamas past the outer walls of Cuz-co's Sacsahuaman fortress. Of the bastion's immense stones, Spanish chronicler Cieza wrote: "It baffles the mind ... how they could be brought up and set in place." Actually, 20,000 men labored 30 years to shape and position the rocks—some weighing more than 100 tons.

CHAPTER FOUR

EIGHT-INCH GOLD-AND-TURQUOISE CHIMU
VESSEL. MUJICA GALLO MUSEUM, LIMA

The

ON JANUARY 24, 1964, veteran mountaineer Erich Groch neared the summit of 20,932-foot Cerro del Toro. The peak dominates a parched wilderness in northwestern Argentina overrun in the 1470's or '80's by the armies of Pachacuti's son, the indefatigable explorer and conqueror Tupa Inca. Just to reach that remote mountain, Groch's expedition had traveled into a lifeless land of salt and sand by jeep for one day, by mule for three, then two on foot. Groch hoped to make the first ascent of the peak.

Sub-zero gales had thwarted an earlier summit attempt, and this time all but one of his companions had dropped out, exhausted and short of breath, at lower altitudes. Close to his goal, Groch stumbled upon the remains of a stone shrine.

Sandal-clad Incas had beaten him to the top by 500 years.

He then spotted a white oval object embedded in weather-shattered rocks. "Antonio!" he shouted. "Pick up that skull!"

"I can't. It's stuck!" his companion replied.

The two men tried to lift it. The skull wouldn't budge. Tossing rocks aside, they uncovered the frozen body of an Indian youth. Naked except for a loincloth, he was huddled facing Cuzco, 1,100 miles to the north. Only the top of his head had been exposed to sun, wind, and snow. His face was in repose, his eyes closed.

Groch replaced the body in its tomb—probably the highest ever found—and returned a month later with archeologist Juan Schobinger and my longtime explorer friend Bernardo Rázquin. After measuring and photographing the site, they backpacked the cadaver down the mountain. It now rests in the university museum at San Juan, Argentina.

"That Indian, about 20, was no peasant," Bernardo told Sue and me. "He had delicate hands and feet. He had been stripped to quicken death by freezing. We could tell by his accouterments that he was a 500-year-old Inca. You know, to touch him really wasn't macabre, it was miraculous!"

Bernardo gave us a list of about 30 peaks ranging from southern Peru to central Chile on which climbers had found Inca remains or relics. "On many summits," he said, "the ancients

Unforgettable One

Crowned by an Inca shrine, cone-shaped Licancábur Volcano juts above Lake Verde on the border between Bolivia and Chile. Pachacuti's son, Tupa Inca Yupanqui—"Unforgettable One"—enfolded this region into the empire during a campaign that ended 1,500 miles from Cuzco on the Maule River, southern border of the Four Quarters of the World.

Overleaf: *Numbed by narcotic coca leaves and streaked with red paint, an Inca youth awaits death by exposure atop a 20,000-foot mountain in the Andes. Priests prepare his rocky crypt. In 1964, mountain climbers discovered a similar sacrifice on El Toro peak in Argentina—a corpse frozen and mummified in high, dry air. Human sacrifices usually commemorated major events—victory in war, an emperor's enthronement.*

offered, instead of children, statues of gold llamas, and silver figurines with miniature wardrobes and headdresses of jungle-bird feathers. They left bundles of wood for beacon fires, antlers, rock walls, even a courtyard at 20,700 feet which had been leveled with nearly 100 tons of earth backpacked from below—about 4,500 loads."

Bernardo told us of frozen human sacrifices found on other peaks. When Sue and I saw one, a boy of 8 or 9, and touched his long eyelashes and his cheeks, we felt the sense of miracle of which Bernardo spoke.

Treasure seekers discovered the frozen child in 1954 on El Plomo peak, in sight of Santiago, Chile. Dr. Grete Mostny, Director of the National Museum of Natural History in Santiago, removed him from a deep-freeze showcase so that I could take his picture. Huddled in his llama-wool tunic, his face painted red with yellow stripes and his feet crossed for warmth like the "mummy" found near El Toro's summit, the boy seemed about to awaken from centuries of sleep. In afterlife, he would not need to hunt for missing parts of his body. Little leather bags at his feet contained hair combings, nail parings, and baby teeth.

"We call him La Momia del Cerro El Plomo," said Dr. Mostny. "But he's more than a mummy; he's flesh and blood—type O, universal donor, as are most full-blooded Indians."

As with the youth found on El Toro peak, the interment of the frozen Chilean boy may date from Tupa Inca's occupation of the region. The emperor's probable route over the Andes from Bolivia to Chile passed in sight of Llullaillaco, at 22,057 feet one of the loftiest volcanoes and archeological sites on earth.

Debris clutters Llullaillaco's icy crown: fallen stone buildings, collapsed roofing, bits of ceramics, basketry, refuse from meals, firewood and ashes, and a sacrificial altar adorned with sacred stones. Llullaillaco even has a stone corral which is still deep in llama droppings.

At the crater's edge lies a log so heavy that modern climbers have reported they were unable to lift it. Perhaps those who tried were weakened by lack of oxygen and the incredible cold of these extreme altitudes, which I learned about firsthand.

One day I flew with Bernardo Rázquin over Aconcagua's 22,834-foot summit, highest in the Americas, a peak not far from El Plomo. Actually, we drifted tailfirst over the top—wind velocity exceeded our 125-knot airspeed. The outside temperature was 31° below zero F.; Bernardo, also a radio weatherman, calculated that the wind dropped the chill factor to 100° below.

These killing temperatures have waylaid scores of Aconcagua

Sacrificed to the sun, an Inca boy sat huddled 500 years on the peak of El Plomo in Chile. Attended by figurines of llamas and a silver goddess, his body now rests inside a freezer-showcase in a Santiago museum.

climbers. On our flight, Bernardo and I had been trying to sight the bodies of two Americans frozen to death months earlier on Aconcagua's eastern glacier at a height about the same as many Inca mountaintop shrines. After the flight I joined six Argentine mountaineer friends to search for the climbers left behind by an ill-fated ten-man expedition.

Twelve days it took us to scale the seldom-climbed eastern approaches with ropes, pulleys, and toboggans for lowering the dead. Gales buffeted our tents, warping the aluminum poles. We muffled our ears and strove to sleep on jagged rock.

One night the wind abated, leaving us in eerie silence on Aconcagua. Our guide unpacked a miniature cassette player. Soon our tent filled with Joaquín Rodrigo's majestic *Concierto de Aranjuez*. Men from the other tent crept into ours. The Spanish guitar and orchestra evoked childhood memories for one climber, the mystique of mountaineering for another. For me, it told of the coming of the Spaniards to this strange New World.

Next day, four of us reached the expedition's uppermost campsite at nearly 20,000 feet, a tatter of tents, food and fuel, and sleeping bags choked with snow at the edge of the glacier. Only 150 yards away we came upon one of those we sought, a U. S. space program engineer. Perfectly preserved, as was the Inca child, he lay staring at the sun. Though handsomely outfitted, he had lost his rope and ice ax, and a crampon was missing from one boot.

I skimmed the engineer's diary for clues to his death. He had thought the ascent would be easy, and wrote of his wife and son: "I sure miss them and wish they could share the trip." At Base Camp he penciled, "I'm saving her letter for . . . the summit."

Entries at Camp II read, "Won't be long before it's all over. Very windy and completely exhausted. . . . For 2¢ I'd go back." At Camp III he made the final entry in a faltering hand: "Supposed to be sheltered from the wind, but nowhere is sheltered."

His wife's letter had been opened. Snow began to fall on the pages as I translated aloud for my friends. It ended, "Keep roped up, and don't forget the crampons, as I don't know how I'd replace you. You are, by far, the best husband and loving one, and really good Dad, in the entire world."

I remember glancing at my three companions and noting that at that great height and in that bitter cold, tears freeze instantly and fall away like pearls.

We strapped the body to a toboggan. The man had weighed about 200 pounds—five times as much as the mummified Inca youth that Bernardo Rázquin backpacked down El Toro—and we would spend three days lowering him 6,000 feet to a snowfield where a helicopter could fly him out.

But first I climbed the glacier alone to search for the other American, a schoolteacher. I found no trace. A sudden blizzard began to obliterate my tracks and drove me downward in mortal fear of finding how it feels to be left to die at 20,000 feet.

At heights so great, memory can falter, judgment fail, and life ebb swiftly, even when one is scientifically outfitted. What, then, enabled lightly-clad Incas not only to survive the night but also to perform elaborate ceremonies? "Was it conditioning, or were they biologically different?" I once asked Bolivian scientists in high country near La Paz which Tupa Inca had annexed to his empire.

I lunched with them at a cosmic ray laboratory 17,000 feet above sea level, close to the upper limit of permanent human habitation. The atmospheric pressure was only about half that of sea level; flames in the fireplace guttered for lack of oxygen.

One scientist—who had grown up in La Paz at 12,000 feet—argued that healthy individuals of all races adjust to such altitudes by natural increase in respiration, lung capacity, and count of red blood corpuscles that pick up oxygen from the lungs.

But I recalled what Father Cobo had written 300 years ago of the Andean Indians' warmbloodedness. "In freezing weather, if you touch their hands, you find them remarkably warm. . . . they sleep by the road wherever night overtakes them, uncovered to the sky; though a palmwidth of snow may fall, they sleep as if in soft beds. I ascribe this extreme warmth to their having stomachs more rugged than the ostrich. . . ." When food is free, Cobo continued, they eat like wolves.

I agreed with the priest that highland Indians convert large quantities of food into body heat. Ignacio, an Aymara Indian scarcely five feet tall who lived with us in La Paz, often ate a gallon of stew at a sitting, and his handshake was warm on the iciest morning. Recalling Ignacio made me wonder whether the rigors of life at great elevations could trigger responses which would be passed on to progeny as new human characteristics.

"Up here there's less atmospheric shielding," said Dr. Ismael Escobar, a nuclear physicist then at the laboratory. "So there're sharper extremes of light and shadow, heat and cold, day and night. And the impact of galactic gamma rays is easier to detect."

Could cosmic rays bring about mutations that could cause genetic change? Did increased radiation from space develop an Inca strain of genius? Or, as English historian Arnold J. Toynbee put it, a "vein of nobility"?

A vein of nobility the great general Tupa Inca certainly possessed. His father, Pachacuti, sent him out to conquer and unify the world. Tupa Inca did so brilliantly, often by sheer Inca prestige and without bloodshed. He took the title Yupanqui, meaning "unforgettable." Yet history has almost forgotten Tupa Inca Yupanqui, while other great conquerors who overran vast regions but failed to unify them ride on in memory.

Tupa Inca rode not a horse but a litter. For perhaps ten thousand miles, blue-liveried bearers of the Rucana tribe matched strides to carry his litter smoothly on their shoulders. His captains also rode, usually in hammocks. His armies walked.

When we followed Tupa Inca's trail of conquest into Argentina and Chile, Sue and I took to the air in a hired plane with a daring and cheerful pilot. He flew us along border volcanoes, and I photographed Inca stonework on exposed crater rims. We saw Indians with bags of flamingo eggs which they had stolen from nests in shallow red, white, and green lakes more than 13,000 feet above sea level. We circled trackless snows, unaware that directly beneath us an Uruguayan plane had crashed months earlier and 16 survivors were subsisting on their deceased fellow passengers.

Winds of more than 100 miles an hour sweep a plume of snow eastward from the crest of 22,834-foot Aconcagua in Argentina, highest mountain in the Western Hemisphere. In November 1973, author McIntyre joined a volunteer team seeking to recover the bodies of two American climbers who froze to death on the peak the preceding January. At the 20,000-foot level, they discovered one frozen body and lashed it to a toboggan (left) for an arduous descent. After an unsuccessful attempt to reach the summit with three companions, the climber had worked his way down a steep glacier alone. Exhausted by the effort and lack of oxygen, and injured in the abdomen from falling on his ice ax, he lapsed into unconsciousness and died—just 150 yards from a high camp with tents and food. A later climbing party found the body of the other American. Centuries before, sandal-clad Incas had scaled mountains nearly as high as Aconcagua to build rock shrines to their gods.

Our little plane also cracked up while taking off in a crosswind on desert sands, but without such desperate consequences. Sue and I, unscathed, continued our quest, while the plane, its wings crumpled, was trundled 1,000 miles on a flatbed truck to its hangar by the now unhappy pilot.

From the Maule River's source in a lofty volcanic basin 170 miles south of Santiago, we traced the river west to Constitución, a seaside resort. Here at the edge of lowland forests, fierce archers had pinned down Tupa Inca's forces a full 3,650 road miles south of lands they had conquered along the Equator.

Despite great distances, the Inca army kept in touch with Cuzco. Thousands of *chasquis* — Inca post runners — relayed throughout the empire verbal messages and quipus knotted with information. Each chasqui knew a stretch of imperial highway roughly two miles long well enough to run it barefoot on a starless night. He carried a sling, the badge and sidearm of Andean man, and sometimes a star-headed mace. During his 15-day spell of duty he lived not far from his home in a beehive-shaped hovel by the road, listening for the call of a conch-shell trumpet that announced a fellow chasqui's approach. The business of empire, and news to and from the capital, moved at about 150 miles a day.

From a surf-drenched Pacific Ocean cliff Sue and I watched Inti, the sun of the Incas, edge into the waves at 9 p.m. to begin his swim under the earth. Along the Maule River, Inti works a 14-hour day in December — though only 10 in June. We wondered whether Inti's behavior at latitude 35° south mystified Inca men of the tropics, accustomed to days and nights of more or less equal length. They had plunged deeper into the Southern Hemisphere than any conquerors in history. Sue thought that perhaps the long winter's night filled them with foreboding. Whatever the reason, they turned back from the Maule after staking out the southern boundary of the Four Quarters of the World.

Once their feet pointed toward Cuzco, the troops surely outdistanced their ambling llama trains. As if in pursuit, but 500 years behind, I hastened to Santiago; Sue flew on to Peru. Crossing the Andes to Mendoza, Argentina, I chased the Inca's wraith along fragments of the royal road. I sought proof of his passage at museums in cities along the highway to Bolivia. Near the border, the complexion of Argentina's people and culture gradually changed from European to Indian.

Above the Tropic of Capricorn, the countryside looked very much like the altiplano near Lake Titicaca. Llamas grazed on yellow ichu grass. Derby-hatted Indian women wore black shawls and skirts of defiant red. Much of Utah-size southwestern Bolivia stretches as flat as the vast prehistoric lake that once covered it, though its plain lies 12,000 feet above sea level. Remaining today are 9,000 square miles of salt deposits — which from the air look like polar ice floes — and saline lakes that with year-end rains may cover 2,000 square miles.

Tupa Inca's armies skirted this wasteland, disinclined to add their skeletons to the brine-bleached bones of lost travelers or to conquer the impoverished Chipaya tribe, whose neighbors held them in contempt. I searched for the lone Chipaya village which

Pierced by a six-foot arrow, an Inca soldier dies at the feet of a forest bowman near the Maule River. Fierce Araucanian tribesmen, armed with such long-range weapons, devastated the Inca slingmen. After four days of rough fighting, they stopped Tupa Inca's thrust to the south.

was virtually undetectable in the middle of a vast open flatland. A swamp said to have surrounded the community in Inca times had dried up, leaving the soil salty-white. For lack of landmarks I lost my way. Darkness fell. Luckily, the headlight beams of my jeep picked out bicycle ruts. They led me long into the night until I came to shapes like giant tombstones that cast shadows in the moonlight.

At first I thought the shapes were *chullpas,* ancient burial towers which stand on the altiplano in the most inexplicable places. Then I heard a baby cry. The shadows belonged to sod houses with rounded thatched roofs and doors of cactus planks. After pounding on door after door, I found lodging with the only resident foreigners in Chipaya: Frances and Ronald Olson, missionaries of the Summer Institute of Linguistics.

Next day I helped Ron clean the house of several inches of dust accumulated during an absence. Half the year, great dust storms abrade the village almost every day. The afternoon ordeal drives Chipayas indoors, so early each morning they begin their field labors: planting quinua with a crude digging stick or driving skinny sheep to brackish water. Older women wash their hair in fermented human urine. Women and girls braid each other's hair into multiple strands like those of the frozen Inca boy.

Despite the efforts of generations of priests and missionaries such as Ron, many Chipaya Indians worship in pagan ways. One deity is the Earth Mother, Pacha Mama, to whom they offer charms in elaborate ritual, kissing the earth. They cherish sacred stones, and revere not only the church tower but also whitewashed cones of sod about four feet high.

The sun's first rays enter doorways of their homes which, like the burial towers, all face east. "Chipayas believe they are the last descendants of the chullpa builders, a people older than the sun," Ron explained. "Their language has interesting similarities to Mayan. They also speak Aymara but no Quechua, having evaded Inca domination—they say. The Chipaya word for 'escape' is the same as 'to win,' which suggests their tribal history."

For better or worse, this isolated community apparently avoided membership in an empire twice as large as Spain and as complicated to govern. To every nation and tribe conquered by the Incas there came from Cuzco a team of administrators which included a quipu expert. They usually governed through local chiefs, imposing the Inca religion and starting work on roads and warehouses. The state took over land, while houses, belongings, and about ten llamas and alpacas remained personal property. Authorities distributed food and garments to the needy, aged, and infirm.

Every five years an inspector—a *tucuyricoc,* "he who sees all" —visited the community and observed its administration. With the governor, he called all the people into a field and divided them into age groups for males and females—from infants to ancients.

A census was taken and noted on quipus. Categories such as herder, soldier, and soothsayer also were recorded, as well as statistics on land, water, and livestock.

The quipus and clay models of the terrain were bundled off to Cuzco along with the most sacred of local huacas. The governor also sent chosen sons and daughters. Inca priests treated the huacas with reverence; teachers guided the children in Inca ways. Yet idols and youngsters both were held hostage so that the Inca capital would become the center of their universe.

Regional officials deported dissidents in exchange for loyal contingents who spoke Quechua. Select tribal groups were transferred to Cuzco, and the provincials settled on the city's outskirts; at this international center, satellite communities housed representatives of the Four Quarters of the World. By law citizens were required to retain regional headdress: wraparound slings, woolen caps with earflaps, nets with dangling cords, and many other styles.

Tribal headmen mastered Quechua, and their young men fought on far frontiers with Inca armies. Subjects adhered to rigid work routines, fearing punishment if they slackened. Though the Incas allowed few luxuries other than additional wives for officials, famine and want were lost to memory.

Few regimes in history have shuffled populations as systematically as the Incas: unruly Ecuadoreans to Peruvian highlands, Titicaca's intractable Aymaras to the Chilean wasteland, Nazca desert dwellers to the Apurimac gorge. Seldom whole tribes, the transferred peoples were mainly malcontents. Hamlets around Copacabana, the lakeshore mecca near the Island of the Sun, still bear names of faraway communities in Peru and Ecuador.

The strategy of population exchange broke up old political units, weakened organized resistance, and brought swift conversion to Inca ways. Emissaries from the Cuzco region spread the language of empire so widely that hundreds of thousands of Quechua names appear on today's detailed maps of Andean countries.

Reigning from Cuzco while Tupa Inca and other sons and captains expanded the empire, Pachacuti perfected the machinery of government. Though allowing some local autonomy and worship, he attempted to control every aspect of the behavior of his subjects. Among the many ordinances recorded on quipus: Mourning for the dead must cease on the twentieth day; women must not touch weapons or musical instruments in time of war; marriages must be ordained and performed in mass ceremonies.

Father Cobo, in a long account of Pachacuti's accomplishments, observed that ". . . Indians honored him more in songs and poems than any other king before or after." As he lay dying, about 1471, Pachacuti recited in a low voice: "Like a lily in the garden I was born, and like a lily I grew up. Years passed, I grew old. I withered, and died."

Suicides joined him, including wives. There were no human sacrifices, for unwilling dead were not welcome. Surgeons embalmed Pachacuti's body. A year passed in mourning festivals, with free viands for all who came to Cuzco. Presently Tupa Inca, who succeeded him, resumed the wars of conquest.

Wielding a wooden club, a Chipaya farmer threshes quinua, a high-protein grain used in making flour and in thickening soups and stews. Sod walls of the circular enclosure block hot, dry gales that each summer afternoon sweep the 12,000-foot-high plain and raise dust thousands of feet into the sky. The remote Chipaya tribe still clings to many of the traditions of its forebears; wearing Inca-style tunics, a family hunkers near their village of domed huts roofed with thatch. A hundred tight, thin braids frame the face of a Chipaya girl—another legacy of Inca Empire fashion. The incessant wind and dry air have chapped her skin.

No profile of Tupa Inca's personality, his strengths and foibles, has been handed down to us, as for Alexander the Great. Tupa Inca lived much longer than Alexander; I conclude that his resistance to disease, intrigue, and self-indulgence was superior to that of the great Macedonian—another unforgettable son who led his father's army to far-flung conquest.

Copper mace head

Chronicles of Tupa Inca's early campaigns, before he became tenth Inca and second emperor, resound with clashing arms, frightful losses, victory, and sometimes retreat. Soldier-historian Cieza's dispatches fairly sing: "The (land of the) Bracamoros he entered and came out fleeing, for it is bad country, that of the jungle." Small wonder: The Bracamoro tribe belonged to the Jívaro headshrinker culture that not even the Spaniards overcame.

Young Tupa Inca was blooded in Chinchaysuyu, the empire's northwest quarter, whose frontiers he pushed to the Equator. His army advanced at a llama's leisurely gait. Unhurried, "he warred more than five moons" around Ayabaca, a brushland border region that I remember as populated mainly by goats. But occupation was swift. "Peace was settled today and tomorrow the province was filled with colonists," Cieza reported. At the town of Tumbes, on the coast, Tupa Inca put on regional clothes to please the natives, a wile familiar to politicians to this day.

Stone mace with ax

The Incas cautioned their troops never to molest the populace, so armies carried all their food and other needs with them on the march. Wives and camp followers must have swollen the size of the army—which Cieza set at 200,000—that defeated the fierce, long-haired Cañari of southern Ecuador. There, in Tomebamba— today's Cuenca—Tupa Inca's sister-wife bore him a son who would become eleventh Inca.

Tupa Inca next turned south and besieged Chan Chan, capital of the Kingdom of Chimor, an immensely wealthy state that controlled 600 miles of Peru's northern coast. The Chimu people revered the moon; to desert dwellers the sun is a destroyer. Chan Chan finally capitulated—by far the most important Inca conquest. The Incas quickly adopted ceremonials from the Chimor kingdom. Goldsmiths, and much of the golden treasure that would arouse Spanish greed, came to Cuzco from the coast.

Then the conqueror took over Pachacamac, a sanctuary 15 miles south of present-day Lima that was dedicated to the earth creator and was the most famous shrine and mecca on the Pacific Coast of South America. Long before Inca times, its oracle attracted pilgrims and dignitaries bearing gifts. Votaries prepared themselves by fasting, then approached the oracle walking backward. Out of unseen mouths of idols or recesses in adobe walls came prophecies uttered in a horrifying hiss. Adopted by the Incas, Pachacamac became the empire's greatest oracle.

South of Pachacamac, Tupa Inca hammered at a desert kingdom and built a garrison whose ruins still command a deep river valley. His highland armies descended this valley to attack the coastal oasis. When he had finally defeated and ceremoniously punished the tenacious coastal nation, the Inca built in Cañete a memorial stronghold. Scarcely 100 years later, Spanish colonists began to cart away its beautifully fitted stones for homes and churches.

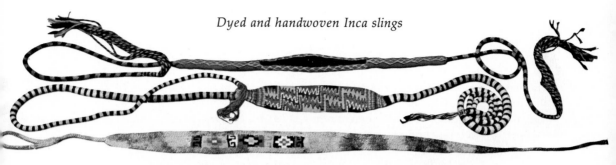

Dyed and handwoven Inca slings

Bone-crushing weapons of war—combined with skilled tactics, shrewd diplomacy, and an awesome reputation—aided Inca armies in the conquest of such powerful foes as the Chimu nation of Peru, guarded by terraced adobe fortresses like La Fortaleza (below). Soldiers armed with brightly patterned slings woven from llama wool hurled stones with deadly accuracy; at other times, they kept their weaponry wrapped around head or waist. A studded mace, swung by a short rope, and a star-shaped mace attached to a staff often proved lethal in close combat. Such weapons caused fractures that Inca surgeons tried to remedy with trepanation—removing part of the cranium (right) with saws, drills, and chisels. Surprisingly, many patients survived.

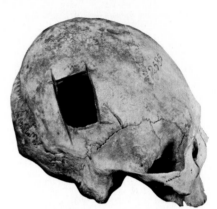

Trepanned Inca skull

Then the rest of the castle that Cieza called "the most graceful and handsome fortress in all the kingdom of Peru" was barged 100 miles north to Callao harbor and dumped to build a breakwater.

After celebrating his consolidation of the coast, Tupa Inca embarked on an adventure northeast of Cuzco that would daunt the hardiest soul today. Crossing the forested ranges to humid flatlands, his armies floated down the broad Madre de Dios River. They may have reached the impassable cataracts on northern Bolivia's far border with Brazil. Natives there once showed me earthworks and pottery bits on the river bank which they insist were left by the Incas on their long expedition.

During this campaign, rumors spread of Tupa Inca's death, and chasquis, unable to carry messages upriver, could not dispel them. A brother, traveling the realm as inspector general, lined up backers in a bid to become Inca. And a Titicaca chieftain, styling himself "Pachacuti Coaquiri," led a widespread uprising.

Then Tupa Inca reappeared and beheaded his upstart brother. He led a powerful army to quell the Titicaca rebellion, and made a drum of Pachacuti Coaquiri's skin. The emperor's armies eventually overran all highland Bolivia, and in Argentina and Chile they conquered an area that doubled the size of the empire.

Tupa Inca envisioned himself master of all the civilized world. He vowed not to stop until he reached the uttermost sea. But when he had first beheld the Pacific Ocean near Manta, Ecuador, he learned that land lay beyond. Sea merchants had arrived on sailing rafts from the islands of Avachumbi and Ninachumbi. Tupa Inca's court necromancer—said to possess the art of flying through the air—verified their existence.

Fascinated, the emperor built a great fleet of balsa-log rafts and ventured into the Pacific with an army of more than 20,000. After about a year he returned with black people, gold, a metal chair, and the hide and jawbone of a horse.

A fanciful sea story? Decades later, it so excited the Spanish viceroy's historian, Captain Pedro Sarmiento de Gamboa, that in 1567 he set sail from Peru for the rumored isles. The expedition discovered the Solomon Islands, but missed Avachumbi and Ninachumbi—which could have been atolls, ring-shaped coral islands, for *chumbi* means "belt" in Quechua.

Authorities call Sarmiento's *Historia de los Incas* "detailed and accurate," though few would argue that Tupa Inca himself made such a voyage. The emperor had brothers and captains with names similar to his who might have done so. However, many skeptics used to insist that American aborigines could not have made transpacific passages on sailing rafts for numerous reasons—the main one being that balsa logs would become waterlogged and sink. Or so they believed until 1947.

In May, June, and July of that year, Peruvian naval officers and I gathered excitedly every day around a Pacific Ocean chart at the naval academy facing Callao harbor. We moved a little flag westward on the chart whenever a position report was radioed by six Scandinavians who had put to sea past our windows on a balsa-log raft, the *Kon-Tiki.* The raft's name ultimately derived from a pre-Inca creator-god named Con-Tici, later prefixed to the name

Descendants of savage warriors, a Shapra Indian man and his son live in the jungle of northeastern Peru, a frontier of the Inca Empire. Here, Tupa Inca's armies encountered tribes of headshrinkers—and fled.

Viracocha—the god who after creating mankind set off across the Pacific from near Manta by walking on the water. Curiously, Tiki is also the aboriginal name of East Polynesia's first human being.

Thor Heyerdahl, builder and skipper of the *Kon-Tiki*, hoped to demonstrate that American Indians could have crossed the Pacific by raft. He didn't fancy that Tupa Inca had sailed the ocean with 20,000 men, although Sarmiento's report indeed helped inspire the *Kon-Tiki* voyage. Thor once exclaimed to me, "What a splendid sight that would have been . . . 400 sailing rafts strung out from horizon to horizon so as to intercept a far-off island!" They might even have been able to return, he contends, for rafts sail well upwind with several adjustable centerboards—an invention that he attributes to South American Indians.

When *Kon-Tiki* sailed out of Callao, my navy friends shook their heads sadly, anticipating that its logs and lashings would soon rot and pull apart in high seas. For weeks we all feared that the little flag we moved across the chart would one day stop to mark the last message from mid-ocean.

On the 101st day *Kon-Tiki* upset the skeptics. Its most serious moment of peril was the landing on a coral-reefed island 4,300 nautical miles away. The success of Thor Heyerdahl's daring adventure proved that Inca sailing rafts could have reached Polynesia and also, in his opinion, that they were safer—though slower—than canoes, and could carry far greater cargoes.

Heyerdahl told me he believed that Sarmiento, in 1567, made a premature course change, thus missing Easter Island, Mangareva, and Timoe, among the nearest populated islands of Polynesia.

"Approaching Mangareva from Peru, he'd have cleared the coral reef that girdles the island through a passage still called Teava-o-Tupa," said Thor. "The Mangareva lagoon until last century sheltered big rafts—with an odd number of logs, pointed at the prow, like *Kon-Tiki*—that sailed to far islands and returned. Mangarevan legends tell of rafts carrying a thousand soldiers to war. Ashore, Sarmiento would have found sweet potatoes called by the same name as in Peru: *kumara*. Too, the Mangarevans preserved a tradition that Chief Tupa once came with a fleet of rafts from a vast and populous land." I find Thor's theories fascinating, although many anthropologists disagree with them.

Heyerdahl also took interest in the seaworthiness of reed boats. In 1970 the adventurous Norwegian scientist made an epic Atlantic crossing from Morocco to Barbados on a large papyrus reed boat, *Ra II*. Again he demonstrated that oceans were not insurmountable barriers to ancient man.

Heyerdahl took Aymara Indian reed-boat builders to Morocco to assemble *Ra II*. They have long since returned to Taquiri, their little island in Titicaca. There they build reed fishing boats to brave storms on the lake where they believe Viracocha created the world. Their ancestors fashioned similar craft that Tupa Inca once boarded to visit temples on the Islands of the Sun and the Moon.

Tupa Inca Yupanqui, the "Unforgettable One," died about 1493. That was the year that Columbus, best remembered of all seafarers, returned to Europe with news that eventually would bring about the fall of the Inca Empire.

Gold raft ferrying a king and his attendants portrays a solemn Chibcha Indian ceremony: Each new ruler, his body dusted with gold, dived into Colombia's Lake Guatavita, washing off his offering to the gods. From this ritual arose the myth of El Dorado—the Gilded One—that to the Spaniards came to signify a magnificent city resplendent with riches.

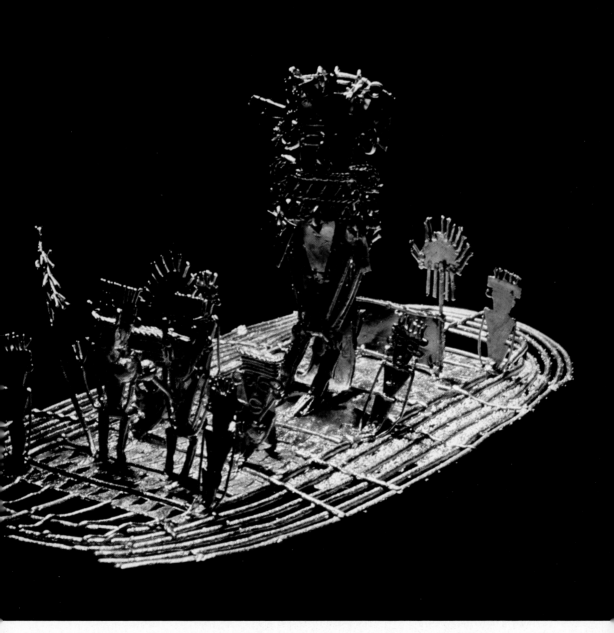

CHAPTER FIVE

EMBOSSED GOLD BREASTPLATE WITH EAR DISKS MADE
BY COLOMBIAN GOLDSMITHS. GOLD MUSEUM, BOGOTÁ

The War

BEFORE SPANIARDS began probing the Pacific Coast of South America early in the 1500's, the Lord Oracle—Apu-Rimac—is said to have foretold the coming of bearded men who would subvert the Inca Empire. Attended by a priestess of Inca lineage, the Lord Oracle dwelt in the Apurimac River gorge that split the realm just west of Cuzco.

It was an appropriate setting for so dire a prophecy. The Apurimac River has cut this chasm thousands of feet into Andean rock. The gorge barred traffic from Cuzco to the Chinchaysuyu—the northwest quarter of the realm—except when October rains came late and the river could be forded. Even then it was dangerous, for few highlanders could swim. From November to May the river thundered. To avoid the gorge by detouring hundreds of miles was impractical and did not meet the requirements of empire.

Neither did the *oroya:* a taut rope supporting a basket pulled back and forth by other ropes. Father Cobo was amused by a 17th-century tightrope artist who, disdaining the basket, pranced across rivers balancing on oroyas. "Indians fled . . . thinking he was a spirit in human form." The oroya is still commonplace.

When Pachacuti pushed Inca rule beyond the Apurimac, he ordered that the river be spanned. Craftsmen spun plant fibers into cables thicker than a man's thigh and built a great suspension bridge. I believe the Incas made people of Curahuasi, a Quechua community high on the far slope, responsible for upkeep and periodic rebuilding of the bridge—just as they gave other tribes special assignments: Cañari as palace guards, Chumbivilcans as court dancers, and Rucanas as litter bearers, the "feet of the Inca."

"The Incas' command was still obeyed in my boyhood," an elder of Curahuasi once told me. But after 450 years of carrying Incas and their haughty Spanish successors across the gorge, the bridge was abandoned in the 1890's and collapsed.

The tumultuous Apurimac might have swept it from the memory of man but for yellowing chronicles and a New Jersey schoolteacher named Thornton Wilder. In 1927, Wilder published a slim novel that began: "On Friday noon, July the twentieth, 1714,

Between the Brothers

Just below the Continental Divide, author McIntyre drinks from the ultimate source of the Amazon River, a lake that now bears his name as leader of the survey team that discovered it. This region, more than one hundred miles south of Cuzco, belonged to the Condesuyu, one of the Four Quarters of the empire inherited by Huayna Capac, son of Tupa Inca.

the finest bridge in all Peru broke and precipitated five travellers into the gulf below." *The Bridge of San Luis Rey* became an American classic and one of the magnets that drew me to Peru.

Part of that attraction lay in the Apurimac itself, for it is the farthest headwater of the Amazon—mightiest of rivers. Because explorers had reported different Amazon sources, I determined to pinpoint once and for all the most remote rivulet of the Apurimac. The National Geographic Society and the Inter American Geodetic Survey sponsored the quest; our expedition left Lima for the Inca heartland in October 1971.

From the little town of Cailloma, we backpacked for three days up an ancient road that finally crossed the Continental Divide at 17,000 feet. Then we traversed an 18,000-foot ridge that led us along an arc of minor peaks forming one of the Apurimac's uppermost catch basins. We climbed mile after mile of summits crowned by wind-carved spires of ice and crumbling rock.

Indians had told us that the Inca name for the crest of the arc was Choquecorao, "Golden Sling." The name appears on Peruvian government topographic maps which one of my companions, Victor Tupa, helped prepare. Victor directs IAGS field parties that verify names of places located by aerial mapping. "We're probably the first to reach this ridge," he declared.

Directly south of Choquecorao the earth fell away so abruptly it seemed that an Inca could have cast a slingstone to the bottom of the Colca River gorge, more than a mile deep. Bound for the Pacific Ocean about 100 miles away, the Colca River has cut a vast ravine lined with one of the most imposing arrays of Inca terraces still under cultivation in all the Andes.

On the north side of Choquecorao, meltwater from ice spires gathers in a little lake. Runoff from this farthest Apurimac source starts a 4,000-mile journey across the continent, its waters mingling with myriad others along the way to form the Amazon—whose volume exceeds the combined flow of the next eight largest rivers on earth. Cascading jungleward, the Apurimac drops some 15,000 feet in 350 miles. During Tupa Inca's expansion of the realm, suspension bridges were built across the Apurimac upstream. On slow-moving lower reaches, the river could be rafted.

At Tupa Inca's death about 1493, one of his younger sons—he fathered 62 in all—was chosen eleventh Inca by the council of long-eared nobles. He received the name Huayna Capac, "Young King." During his coronation and simultaneous marriage to his sister, Cuzco erupted with joy. Citizens representing many tribes dressed in finest raiment. Priests scattered feathers on walls and roofs, and sprinkled golden nuggets in the streets. Prison doors were opened. Huayna Capac had grown up in a regency of family nobles including his mother, Mama Ocllo. A strong-willed queen, she advised her son and influenced his decisions. Not until she died did Huayna Capac set forth in godlike splendor to inspect his Tahuantinsuyu, the Four Quarters of the World. He put down uprisings, exchanged populations, replaced governors, provisioned garrisons, constructed fortresses and pleasure palaces, and favored loyal allies with women and fine clothing.

Huayna Capac found most of his realm's frontiers circumscribed by barbarians and inhospitable lands unworthy of conquest. In Bolivia he clashed with naked Chiriguano Indians on the eastern frontier, but did not pursue them into humid swamplands. In Argentina he halted at the edge of the Andes, for salt flats to the east were probably even less inviting than Bolivian swamps. In Chile he decided, as had his father, to leave the Araucanian Indians alone in their dark pine forests south of the Maule River.

The empire's eastern frontier melted into wilderness; the western was etched for thousands of miles by the breakers of Mama Cocha, Mother Sea. Between the two extremes, the young emperor toured the Four Quarters accompanied by his entourage, receiving homage and gifts of beautiful concubines, until he possessed perhaps 600. Subjects worshiped him as divine. But most of the realm belonged to his dead ancestors and their legatees.

Pachacuti had ordained that wealth derived from conquered lands became the property of each Inca and that it could be inherited only by that Inca's mummy, his personal idols, and his direct descendants—excepting the new emperor. Thus, each new ruler had to make his own fortune, mainly by war. But many years of travel and campaigning must have convinced Huayna Capac that his father and grandfather had conquered all the world worth having—except the north with its rich goldsmithing cultures. And so Huayna Capac turned toward Ecuador and Colombia around 1515. As customary before every grave decision or call to war, the Inca prayed, sought favorable auguries, and consulted oracles. Apparently neither soothsayer nor oracle warned Huayna Capac that his sojourn would last more than a decade and that he would never again see Cuzco—for he would come home a mummy.

The emperor called "two hundred thousand men of war" to arms, according to Cieza. The levy was readily met because of the accurate census and close control of the populace by officials who supervised taxpayers in multiples of 10 up to 10,000. The mobilization also would have the effect of a religious crusade, in spreading the gospel of the Creator and the Sun.

Troops camped around the capital. The usual ceremonies likely ensued, ending only when everyone was overcome with drink. Before major battles, mummies of Inca rulers and huacas of conquered tribes were displayed in the great square, and each mummy's bard celebrated his Inca's historic deeds in song. Priests sacrificed thousands of llamas, burned huge quantities of fine clothing, and offered feather and shell ornaments to the sun.

Boys and girls from all the realm, splendidly adorned, circled the plaza. The handsomest were chosen for *capacocha*—human sacrifice—in Cuzco. Others, selected for sacrifice to regional deities, set out for the Four Quarters. Their immolation took place on distant peaks, in caves and rivers, and other dwellings of gods. Unless such gods were attended to, their wrath might be aroused against the Inca.

Carving its mile-deep gorge, the Apurimac River presents an awesome barrier to travelers heading west from Cuzco. Its waters foam through rapids and whirlpools, dropping 15,000 feet in 350 mountainous miles; then the current slows and broadens. For centuries before the rise of the Inca Empire, people scrambled down steep canyon walls and crossed the river in a basket suspended from a rope. Using this technique, an Ecuadorean Indian (below), his hair plastered with red achiote-seed paste, pulls a wooden platform along a cable. Under Pachacuti's orders, Curahuasi villagers living along the gorge of the Apurimac built a switchbacking trail down to the river. They spun and secured a bridge of fiber-rope 150 feet long. Sturdy and supple, it conveyed Inca emperors, emissaries, armies, and llama trains on missions to and from the capital.

Jungle mist and a scattering of light mark a new day for Aguaruna Indians paddling a dugout on the Santiago River in northern Peru. In this region east of the Andes—one of the rainier areas on earth—tribes of headshrinkers armed with bows and arrows repelled the Incas. But highland hunters still raided the jungles seeking the pelts of rare animals like the jaguar and the plumage of birds like the macaws drifting above the forest crown (above). From feathers of brilliant colors and from tawny hides spotted with black, artisans made ceremonial clothing for Incas.

Huayna Capac's troops with their camp followers must have taken weeks to file out of Cuzco. Cieza wrote that the Inca "carried with him 2,000 women and left in Cuzco more than 4,000." He also took two sons: his heir Ninan Cuyuchi, and a favorite, Atahuallpa. I can visualize the splendor of that imperial procession.

If peasants hoeing potatoes dared lift their eyes, or perhaps came running with the gift of a twinned ear of corn, they might not view their lord, for his litter was often curtained — though it had peepholes to see out. But a halt at Anta — Xaquixaguana in the chronicles — allowed scurrying tambo attendants to glimpse the Son of the Sun. The tambo was a storehouse-barracks that rural communities maintained apart from the populace to feed and quarter travelers on official business.

From Xaquixaguana a broad causeway led the royal party straight across five miles of quagmire. Pressing on, litter bearers came to Tarahuasi, a tambo and ceremonial center whose walls of polygonal stones, orange with lichens, still stand beside the high road into the Apurimac gorge. There the Inca spent the night, sleeping, like his subjects, on a simple mat.

Next, the procession switchbacked mile after mile down to the Apurimac. "It was like descending the coils of a flattened corkscrew," wrote E. George Squier, a North American archeologist who made the descent in the 1860's. "The gorge narrowed . . . until it was literally shut in by precipices of stratified rock strangely contorted; while huge masses of stone, rent and splintered as from some terrible convulsion of nature, rose sheer before us, apparently preventing all exit from the sunless and threatening ravine, at the bottom of which a considerable stream struggled, with a hoarse roar, among the black boulders."

Near the bottom, the highlanders' senses swam in the hot and thickening air, cactus spines punctured their bare legs, and sand flies feasted on them mercilessly. So voracious were the insects that neither the flapping of a feather parasol nor divine intercession kept them away from the tender earlobes and eyelids of the Son of the Sun. He shared the discomfort of his vassals as blood-reddened sweat coursed his beardless cheeks.

Perhaps Huayna Capac halted at a cliffside temple to consult Apu-Rimac, the Lord Oracle. The oracle's effigy was a tree trunk, the size of a human body, that was splashed with sacrificial blood. Father Cobo records that it had "a golden belt one palm wide, with two women's breasts of solid gold. . . . Next to this idol were other smaller ones . . . bathed with blood and dressed like women." The oracle's guardian, a hag of royal blood, kept to the shadows while incanting her prophecies. When the Spaniards came, the witch "threw herself from the cliff . . . calling on her god Apurimac."

The explorer Squier wrote: "swinging high in a graceful curve, between the precipices on either side, looking wonderfully frail and gossamer-like, was the famed bridge of the Apurimac," whose crossing he vowed never to forget. By day the bridge yellowed in the sun, a most unlikely conduit for mighty armies. By night it swayed like a giant's empty hammock, buffeted by gusts that shrieked down from lofty snows.

As the royal litter ventured onto a footing of twigs 120 feet

Quito's buildings gleam silver-white on a plateau between the summit of Pichincha Volcano and a valley of green fields. In Ecuador, highland hamlets like the one at left have changed little since Huayna Capac established Quito as the empire's northern capital. He remained in Ecuador's mild climate for some ten years; about 1527 he died of plague, and the empire broke into two sectors.

Celebrating Yamor—thanksgiving for the harvest—villagers in Otavalo, Ecuador, re-enact the arrival of an Inca emperor with a vanguard of Chosen Women. Watching from the sidewalk, nine-year-old Luz Maria Pichamba wears a scarf in Inca tradition and a tribal necklace of brass beads. Huayna Capac, extending his empire north of Quito and beyond the Colombian border, subdued the Otavalans with difficulty and barely succeeded in crushing a bitter revolt. The tribe—renowned as weavers even in Inca times—now sells softly napped wool blankets and ponchos throughout the world.

above the current, the bridge sagged and surged giddily; bearers had to break their stride to dampen the swells. They clambered up the far side and wove their way through several hundred feet of intermittent tunnel carved in rock. That night the Inca might have lodged at Curahuasi, high on the west bank. Beside the road stood storehouses stuffed with food, clothing, and weapons.

Before daybreak whitened the icy fog that clung to the treeless backbone of the Andes, scouts ran ahead to proclaim the Inca's coming and ranged the countryside to bring back intelligence. Chasquis sped messages up and down the line of march, as well as to and from Cuzco. The next settlement, Abancay, was the main home of the Quechua people; they spoke the language which by Inca edict had become the *runa simi*—man's speech. It eventually displaced almost a hundred tribal tongues. Pachacuti had made his trusted Quechua allies "Incas by privilege."

"The Indians cleaned all the road so that no blade of grass or stone was seen..." wrote Cieza of the Inca's travels. "And so many people went to see him that it seemed that all the hills and slopes were full of them; and all called down blessings... '*Ancha hatun apu, intipchuri*... great and powerful lord, Son of the Sun...' little short of adoring him as God."

Cieza noted that many came out to serve the Inca, carrying baggage from one town to the next. Today the heavily laden foot traveler in the hinterlands must still seek the aid of bearers. It can be costly to bargain your way out of remote villages when you are not the Inca. But you *can* ride a rattly bus close by the route that Huayna Capac followed to the isolated sun temple of Vilcas, the Viracocha temple at Jauja that once had more than 8,000 attendants, and Tarma with its oracle and a sun god the natives called Mocha.

Today's highway runs on north to the city of Huánuco, while the old royal road climbs high into the mountains to a vast and desolate ruin of cut stone. In Huayna Capac's time, this place bustled with 30,000 public servants as a provincial capital and staging area for the northern campaigns.

From here the regal procession entered a region of overwhelmingly jumbled topography: the magnificent escarpment between Peru's Cordillera Blanca, which rises to 22,205 feet, and the Marañón River gorge—one of the longest and deepest trenches on any continent. Sometime during his travels, the emperor crossed the Marañón northeast of Cajamarca to make his first conquest of new land in the humid forests around Chachapoyas and Moyabamba, where the Chancas had taken refuge from his ancestors.

Huayna Capac's arrival in Tomebamba—now Cuenca, Ecuador—was a homecoming, for he had been born there during Tupa Inca's northern campaign. He built himself a palace with walls brightly painted and inlaid with mother-of-pearl. In its sanctum, a golden huaca of Mama Ocllo held Huayna Capac's placenta.

In Tomebamba, free of the constraints imposed by Cuzco's nobles, the emperor indulged in drinking bouts and, according to Garcilaso, "was unable to deny a woman anything, whatever her age, rank, and appearance." He would, the writer went on, lay his right hand on her left shoulder and say, "Mother [or sister, or daughter], whatever you wish."

But the goldsmithing nations and new lands to conquer for his own estate lay farther north, some of them beyond the Equator. Halfway there from Tomebamba the mountain road vanished under a quicksand of fine black ash, which was still drifting across the highway. Inca soldiers must have floundered. By day they could take their bearings from continuously erupting Sangay, originator of the ash, and by night from lava glowing on the snowy flank of its cone. Continuing north, the line of march threaded a corridor of solitary snowcapped volcanoes: Tungurahua, Capac Urcu, Chimborazo, Cotopaxi. Each was a great deity. At 9,350 feet on the flank of twin-cratered Pichincha, Huayna Capac established Quito as the empire's northern bastion.

Beyond Quito, fierce Ecuadorean resistance shattered Peruvian aplomb. In Tomebamba's rich court the Inca held absolute sway, but death took command on the northern frontier and irrigated the lush slopes with Inca blood. Unyielding Pasto Indians blunted the southerners' thrusts into thickly populated Colombia.

Huayna Capac finally abandoned attempts to overcome the goldsmithing cultures when Ecuadoreans in his wake revolted. The vengeance he inflicted on one tribe is commemorated in the name of a lovely lake, Yaguarcocha, just north of the Equator. One day as Sue and I trolled its blue waters our boatman remarked that Yaguarcocha means "bloody lake." He added with surprising bitterness: "Its waters were reddened by the blood of my ancestors whom the Peruvians massacred."

About 25 miles north of the present-day Ecuador-Colombia border, the emperor marked the empire's northern boundary with golden stakes driven into the banks of the Angasmayo, "Blue River." Inca influences reached beyond the markers, however. At the headwaters of the Putumayo River, a major tributary of the Amazon, Indians richly robed in red ponchos once told me that their tribal name was "Inga." They belonged to the Quillacinga ("Moon Nose") nation, named for golden nose ornaments up to two feet wide, that were shaped like half-moons.

"Moon Noses," Incas called Indians of Colombia who wore gold nose ornaments shaped like half-moons; this one measures six inches across.

GOLD MUSEUM, BOGOTÁ

Huayna Capac also annexed the hot Ecuadorean littoral, though betrayal by cannibals of Puná Island in the Gulf of Guayaquil blighted his dreams of conquest. The Puná chief, Tumbala, had pretended to submit; he feted ornamented Inca noblemen and agreed to raft them to the mainland. At sea, recorded Cieza, "the islanders treacherously slipped the ropes that bound the logs of the rafts, so that the poor long-ears fell into the water, where with great cruelty they were killed with secret weapons" carried by the islanders. Excellent swimmers, the Puná seamen looted the corpses, reassembled the rafts, and went back to embark more highlanders—until all were dead. Huayna Capac ordered bards to memorialize the tragedy in mournful song, said Cieza.

The Inca had suffered other reverses, among them mutiny by his legions. Only a last-minute appeal by a priestess dissuaded them from marching home to Cuzco—which had become a city of priests and bureaucrats more than 1,300 miles removed from the seat of imperial power. But despite his problems and long absence from Cuzco, Huayna Capac was content in Tomebamba, "a land so serene that . . . none outdoes it in all this realm."

Still, bad omens beset the Inca. Three large halos encircled the moon. Lightning struck the palace. The earth quaked more often than usual; mountains collapsed. Tides rose higher than normal. A sick eagle fell from the sky. A comet appeared and it was green. One midnight, Huayna Capac imagined he saw thousands of silent ghosts surrounding him.

"One day Huayna Capac was taking his ease at his palaces in Tomebamba . . ." Father Cobo wrote, when "awed and frightened messengers reported that strange people never before seen had landed on the beach at Tumbes . . . they were white, they had beards and fierce looks . . . they traveled by sea in great wooden houses . . . where they slept by night . . . and by day they went ashore; and by gestures asked to see the lord of the land. . . .

"The Inca was stunned upon hearing these things, and fell into such apprehension and melancholy that he went alone into his chambers and did not come out until nearly night. Then other chasquis sent by the governors on the coast told how the strangers had entered the royal houses and palaces . . . carried off all their treasures . . . and weren't afraid to go into the den where the Inca kept his beasts. Huayna Capac, shaken and beside himself . . . called the messengers back to repeat what had happened. They said, 'Lord . . . the lions and wild animals you have in your palaces crouched on the ground before them and wagged their tails as if they were tame.'

"The Inca, very wrought up, rose from his stool and, shaking his cloak, said, 'Get out! Get out, nobles and soothsayers. Don't disturb and trouble my realm and authority.' And sitting down on another stool, he bade the emissaries to retell the matter again and again, not quite believing it for its bizarreness and strangeness."

The houses sailed away, leaving two men at Tumbes. Huayna Capac ordered them brought before him. But apparently he never saw the strangers who wore silver jackets and bore sticks that spoke the thunder; they disappeared from history.

A chronicler also tells of a black-cloaked chasqui who brought Huayna Capac a small casket. When the Inca opened it, moths and butterflies flew out, spreading a plague. The virulent casket was a myth, but the plague was not. The emperor's sister-wife and his brother and uncle who governed Cuzco had already died in an epidemic that took an estimated 200,000 lives. Possibly it was smallpox transmitted to the New World by Europeans.

About 1527, Huayna Capac was stricken in Quito. Twice he named an heir and twice his priests performed the *calpa* ceremony —divination by examining llama viscera. The omens were inauspicious for crown prince Ninan Cuyuchi; he soon died of plague.

Gaining revenge against their captors, Puná Island cannibals slip the lashings of log rafts and murder Inca nobles whom they had promised to ferry to the Ecuadorean mainland. The islanders then looted the bodies.

Soldiers of Atahuallpa's armies drag Emperor Huascar from his royal litter. Civil war raged between the half-brothers after the death of their father Huayna Capac. Atahuallpa eventually had his rival executed.

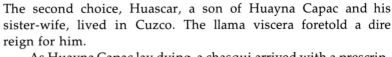

The second choice, Huascar, a son of Huayna Capac and his sister-wife, lived in Cuzco. The llama viscera foretold a dire reign for him.

As Huayna Capac lay dying, a chasqui arrived with a prescription from the powerful Oracle of Pachacamac: Expose the Inca to the sun. The treatment failed. Under the equatorial rays of his celestial ancestor, death came to the last of three absolute monarchs—father, son, and grandson—who ruled a unique universal state for nearly a century.

Upon Huayna Capac's death, "so great was the weeping that . . . birds fell stupefied from the sky," wrote Cieza, recording the stories of those who were there. As the funeral procession wound its way to Cuzco, mourners from remote villages climbed hills to view the passing of the golden sun image and the emperor's mummy—richly dressed and armed as if he were alive. On such occasions, devout Indians plucked eyebrow hairs as votive offerings and blew them into the air.

Cieza's informants said that "In Cuzco . . . more than 4,000 souls were put to death . . ." to be buried with Huayna Capac. The high priest conferred the imperial fringe on Huascar, the first of five sons of Huayna Capac who would become reigning Incas.

Atahuallpa, one of Huascar's scores of half-brothers and the ruler of Quito, did not accompany his father's mummy to Cuzco. Not deigning to pay homage to the new emperor, he stayed in Quito. With him remained hardened Inca armies he had often led into battle, and their generals: Quisquis, Chalcuchima, Rumiñahui, and other famed veterans of the Ecuadorean wars.

When summoned to Cuzco, Atahuallpa instead sent messengers with presents. Huascar cut off their noses and returned some of the vassals with an insulting gift of women's clothes for Atahuallpa. Knowing then that his reward for fealty to Huascar would be death, Atahuallpa, at the urging of his captains, proclaimed himself King of Quito—a state separate from the empire.

Years passed before Huascar decided to dispatch an army of largely inexperienced conscripts against his insurgent half-brother. The emperor's men perished in battle near Ambato, Ecuador, and Atahuallpa ordered their skeletons stacked as a war memorial. Cieza saw the grisly battleground about 20 years later and wrote, ". . . from the amount of bones, even more must have died than the count . . . of 15 or 16 thousand Indians."

Victory at Ambato revolutionized Atahuallpa's strategy. The King of Quito ordered Generals Quisquis and Chalcuchima to engage and capture Huascar with their experienced troops. Battling south, they cleared the way to Cuzco, destroying army after army that Huascar had recruited from the farthest reaches of the Tahuantinsuyu: from Peru, Bolivia, Chile, Argentina, and the Amazon jungle. Tens of thousands of farmer-soldiers who had escaped the plague now fell under the northerners' onslaughts. Atahuallpa's soldiers eventually reached the Apurimac gorge.

Atahuallpa still watched from Ecuador, and Huascar had not taken to the field. Despite conflicting advice of nobles, priests, and oracles, Huascar did personally lead troops of many provinces, each in distinctive costume, across Apurimac bridges to the far side of the gorge. A chronicler described the spectacle. "Huascar climbed the highest Apurimac crest and rejoiced to see men numerous as sand. Mountains, valleys, and plains were covered with gold and silver and plumage of a thousand colors. . . . The peoples of each province beat drums, played instruments, and sang war songs . . . they say it was a thing to cause people to take leave of their senses."

One of the greatest battles in Inca history followed, a struggle in which, chroniclers said, more than 150,000 Indians died. It was the final conflict in the War Between the Brothers. The gods at first seemed to favor Huascar. By setting fire to dry grass, he burned the greater part of the forces of Quisquis and Chalcuchima. But instead of pursuing victory, he made the beginner's mistake of stopping for the night and celebrating.

The crafty Quito generals planned an ambush and gathered their troops in the dark. In the morning, Huascar rode into the trap. Well-thrown bolas ensnared the legs of litter bearers. General Chalcuchima dragged the Son of the Sun to the ground. Chalcuchima, a grand master of terror, then rode Huascar's litter into the defenders' camp. When they recognized the scourge from the north, the demoralized soldiers fled and probably did not stop until they reached their homes in far corners of the Tahuantinsuyu.

Atahuallpa's armies crossed the undefended Apurimac bridges and marched on Cuzco. They sacked the city, desecrating Tupa Inca's palace and burning his mummy, for his adherents had backed Huascar. To erase the past, they burned the quipus and killed quipu camayocs. One chronicler said that they dressed Huascar in women's clothes and fed him excrement. They forced him to witness the extermination of his multitudinous harem and his courtiers; three of Huayna Capac's sons managed to escape.

On his way from Ecuador to make a triumphal entry into Cuzco, Atahuallpa consulted the Oracle of Huamachuco, which predicted he would come to a bad end. Enraged, Atahuallpa struck off the head of the Oracle's guardian, an old priest whose robe was decorated with seashells. About this time, chasquis brought word that bearded men—like those who had stepped ashore some five years earlier—had reappeared. Curious to see the silver-jacketed strangers, their beasts, and their magic staves that commanded thunder and lightning, Atahuallpa broke his journey to Cuzco. He had sent emissaries to consult Pachacamac, greatest of oracles, near present-day Lima. That oracle now advised Atahuallpa not to fear the foreigners; all would die.

When word of the strangers reached faraway Cuzco, the capital's ravaged citizens found new reason for hope. They had offered anguished prayers to their supreme being, Viracocha, for deliverance from Atahuallpa. After the creation, they knew, Viracocha had set off across the ocean from near Manta, Ecuador, walking on the waters. People believed that he would return in time of crisis. Surely the bearded ones were sent by Viracocha to save the Inca Empire!

Frosted Sangay Volcano, a landmark to Inca armies marching through the mountains west of it, towers above sultry jungle southeast of Quito. Sangay continues to erupt, covering the ground with fine black ash.

CHAPTER SIX

Invaders

GOLD NECKLACE FROM PERU WEIGHING ALMOST
TEN OUNCES. MUJICA GALLO MUSEUM, LIMA

IN NOVEMBER 1532, a steel-helmeted column of 62 cavalrymen, 105 foot soldiers, and a priest wound into the mountains of northern Peru to confront the Inca Atahuallpa. Francisco Pizarro, an aging adventurer both unlettered and illegitimate, led the column. His coat of arms displayed a llama; his title, Governor and Captain General of Peru, had been granted by King Charles I of Spain — though Peru was not his and he had little notion that it was twice the size of his own country. Nor did Pizarro, for that matter.

His companions included four younger half-brothers. Hernando *was* legitimate and literate. Juan, Gonzalo, and Martín stemmed from various unwed parents — Martín's last name was de Alcántara. An old conquistador who knew them all penned a succinct family portrait: They were "... *tan soberbios como pobres, é tan sin hacienda como deseosos de alcanzarla* — as proud as they were poor, and as much without wealth as eager to achieve it."

Pizarro's dashing cavalry captain, Hernando de Soto, would later invest a weighty share of Inca treasure in exploring North America. There he would discover the Mississippi River, ultimately his grave. Several other followers had won minor titles for brave deeds on Pizarro's two earlier expeditions in searching for the Inca Empire. And each of them hungered for the title of hidalgo — *hijo de algo*, "somebody."

Their armament, besides lances and Toledo blades, consisted of a few crossbows and arquebuses and one or two small cannon. A number of coastal Indian auxiliaries and bearers accompanied them. Despite ten years' planning and exploring, Pizarro's invasion of the Inca Empire was ridiculously undermanned. Atahuallpa, accustomed to commanding huge armies, must have been more mystified than awed to hear of it.

Atahuallpa then had traveled halfway from Quito to Cuzco for a ceremony to confirm him as fifth emperor of Tahuantinsuyu, the Four Quarters of the World. He had encamped at Cajamarca, a flat 9,000-foot-high valley enclosed by rounded mountains too low for snow; there he could receive his visitors with appropriate pomp.

The Incas had taken Cajamarca during the reign of Pachacuti, Atahuallpa's great-grandfather. There they had installed a luxurious complex of baths around thermal springs which bubbled

from an Alien World

Point of embarkation for the New World, the inland port of Seville, Spain, teems with adventurers dreaming of conquest and merchants seeking profit. Conquistador Francisco Pizarro sailed from here in 1502.

"VISTA DE SEVILLA," ATTRIBUTED TO SÁNCHEZ COELLO, MUSEO DE AMÉRICA, MADRID

Outpost of empire, the crumbling citadel of Incallacta— once garrisoned by Inca warriors armed with slingstones —guarded the easternmost frontier of Bolivia against incursions by cannibals from the swampy flatlands. Then, the monumental fortress dominated access roads slicing through the mountains; today, few visitors journey to this isolated region, about two hundred miles southeast of La Paz. At right, the adobe of an ornamental niche, topped by a heavy stone lintel, still shows the original red paint.

from the eastern edge of the valley and flowed in steaming rills through its meadows. Courtiers and wives attended the Inca in sumptuous splendor. Bright tents of his army—eyewitnesses estimated it variously from 30,000 to 80,000 men—blanketed the mountains, although his best troops were pillaging Cuzco, nearly a thousand road miles away.

Atahuallpa sent a noble emissary with gifts—embroidered vicuña cloth, two pottery castles—to invite the Spaniards to Cajamarca. The noble came upon De Soto coolly reconnoitering the mountain highway a hundred miles inland, in the wake of the War Between the Brothers: Executed soldiers hung by their heels at the roadside; towns were depopulated. De Soto gladly escorted the emissary to Pizarro, who anxiously awaited the patrol's return.

After entertaining and quizzing his noble visitor, Pizarro sent him back to Atahuallpa with a fine shirt and two goblets of Venetian glass. Then, knowing full well that the Inca was encamped amidst an army, the Spaniards nevertheless resumed their cautious march inland.

How did those 168 Europeans come by the colossal nerve to invade an empire of six million inhabitants? What drew them into such a splendidly illogical, if not suicidal, adventure? Was it simply gold? Or more than that?

The Spaniards' hunger for the yellow metal puzzled natives, who wondered whether the Europeans ate it. Indians did not grasp at first the alien concept that gold was not wanted for itself but for what it could buy; that Spanish soldiers lucky enough to find it did not hoard treasure but were prodigal spenders who "bought pigs in a sow's belly before they were born," as Cieza put it.

Avarice was but one of their compulsions. The Spaniards also were driven by a monumental faith honed in holy war against the Moors—Muslims who had occupied Spain for 700 years. For many, the conquest was a crusade. They called themselves "Christians" more often than Spaniards, and some referred to the Indians as "Moors" and their temples as "mosques." If they lost their wild gamble and their lives, was it not in service of the Cross?

"The daring of the Spaniards is so great that nothing in the world can daunt them," wrote Cieza, stating fact, not boast. "No other race can be found which can penetrate through such rugged lands ... solely by the valor of their persons and the forcefulness of their breed ... without bringing with them wagons of provisions ... or tents in which to rest, or anything but a sword and a shield, and a small bag in which they carried food."

But they did bring along their cherished horses, which vastly extended each individual's mobility and power, and a few firearms, clumsy and of dubious value. Mounted men were to prove far more effective than musketeers in the conquest.

The leader of the column bound for Cajamarca possessed ruthless single-mindedness and self-confidence. In age, experience, and resourcefulness, as well as uncommon resistance to disease, he was the archetypal conquistador. Francisco Pizarro and many of his followers came from Extremadura, the harsh frontier of west-central Spain. His hometown, Trujillo, lay directly north of Seville, main port of embarkation for the New World. Pizarro had reached manhood by 1492, when the Moors were finally driven from Spain. Unemployed adventurers roamed the country lusting to be "somebody." Poor but haughty, they had untrammeled egos and reckless faith in themselves, bowing only to God and King. By instinct and training they were so aggressive that their natural response to danger was instant, murderous attack.

They strove to emulate the supermen of the adventure stories spawned by medieval holy wars. In 1490 the recently invented printing press had begun turning out book after book of chivalric romances, the fantasy fiction of those times. In rambling tales of exploits in imaginary lands, heroes hacked through incredible odds to gain gold and glory—and love so rapturous that they swooned at the mere mention of their lady's name.

The best-known Spanish literary character of the day, Amadís de Gaula, was "the one knight errant above all others," according to Don Quixote. The *Amadís de Gaula* cycle ran more than 20 volumes, thousands of battle-saturated pages, even including aerial combat: A knight bestride a griffin dueled a flying dragon.

Spanish gentlemen were encouraged to imitate the chivalrous manners of Amadís, an armored rider clever at languages and a master of cunning strategy. Combat was the only way to win honor. Without honor, mere survival was meaningless. Against astronomical odds, Amadís fought scores of pagan kings. In one contest, three knights took on an army of 235,000, though shrewder heroes enlisted allies. The number of heathen converted was bettered only by the number killed.

The discovery of the New World made such fantasies almost come true. Conquistadors recalled the bellicose "Black Amazons of Californie" —in Book V of *Amadís*—when they fought skirted warriors on the banks of the great river that rises in Inca territory. And Bernal Díaz del Castillo, chronicler of the conquest of Mexico, wrote upon sighting the Aztec capital in 1519: ". . . when we saw so many cities and villages built in the water and other great towns on dry land and that straight and level causeway running to the city,

Francisco Pizarro: illiterate and illegitimate, iron-willed and single-minded. Backed by titles from the Spanish Crown, the conquistador mounted three expeditions to find and conquer the Inca Empire.

we were amazed and said it was like the enchantments we had read of in *Amadís de Gaula* on account of the great towers and *cues* [temples] and buildings rising from the water. . . ."

Francisco Pizarro, then in Panama city, heard the stirring news. He had accompanied Vasco Nuñez de Balboa across the Isthmus of Panama in 1513. On the Pacific shore they learned of a land of gold and long-necked "Peruvian sheep"—or were they camels? Balboa built ships to probe south but was beheaded by his rival, the Governor of Panama, before he could search for the empire then ruled by the Inca Huayna Capac.

A European had indeed set foot in Huayna Capac's domain a decade before Pizarro. One Aleixo Garcia survived a shipwreck on Brazil's Atlantic Coast in 1516 and later pushed into the unknown continent. Supported by savage Chiriguano Indians, he and his countrymen raided the central Bolivian province of Charcas in the early 1520's. Their transcontinental trek in quest of Inca booty was comparable to marching on Kansas from Cape Cod, a century before the Pilgrims landed at Plymouth Rock.

Inca defenders turned Garcia back short of fabulous riches and a firm place in history. He perished on the return trip. Word of his reported "kingdom of silver," which would give rise to the name Argentina, was long in reaching Spain, and his exploit was largely ignored by the chroniclers of Peru.

The end of the Inca Empire began inauspiciously in November 1524, when Francisco Pizarro sailed from Panama bound for Peru — wherever that might be. Not knowing, he felt his way down the inhospitable Colombian coast against prevailing winds and currents. He skirted jungled slopes that rose steeply out of the Pacific and shed rain in countless streams. Then he poled through a mangrove maze where tides flushed gray mud in and out of shallow rivers and estuaries. Sea, shore, and sky merged into murk without horizon along that thousand-mile coastline, where rainfall could reach 300 inches a year.

Today the coast's few inhabitants swelter in isolated lumberyards, small towns, and one sultry city, Buenaventura. They are friendly folk. Many natives of Pizarro's day, however, were cannibals. His soldiers suffered from Indian arrows, heat rash under wet armor, and intestinal cramps from unknown berries gulped down when food ran out. Many died.

Knee-deep mud sucked at their rotting boots as they marched blindly inland. Painted savages wounded Pizarro seven times in a single engagement. The invaders did not penetrate far enough to contact the Quimbaya, finest goldsmiths in the New World. Far short of elusive Peru, they turned back.

Loath to face creditors and the Governor of Panama in such a sorry state, Pizarro and his men avoided Panama city until wounds healed, flesh fattened, and the governor's wrath at such waste of lives and supplies subsided. Then, as if his disastrous expedition had succeeded, Pizarro made a private contract to conquer and divide Peru and share its spoils equally with two partners who had sponsored his first expedition. They were Fernando de Luque, a churchman who raised money, and Diego de Almagro, a tough old soldier who raised fighting men. They still knew almost nothing of an empire ruled by an all-powerful Inca.

Manpower and supplies had dwindled on the Pacific side of the Isthmus, for gold and glory had beckoned everyone to Mexico, and the Governor would not permit recruiting for Peru's invasion until paid his share of the spoils in advance. Not until 1526 could Pizarro get his second expedition under way. Two caravels then

"Here Pizarro landed!" shouts Jovita, only inhabitant of the Isle of the Rooster. On this shore the conquistador challenged his men, dispirited by setbacks, to risk toil, famine, and death in pursuit of Inca riches.

Shaped by master craftsmen, treasures of ancient goldwork radiate the styles of Colombian artists. These artifacts, found buried in tombs hidden from conquistadors, survive as prized museum pieces. Now chipped and disfigured, the nine-inch-tall image of a seated person probably represents a deity. The nine-inch flask with decorative knobs and the six-inch fluted container with a golden chain each held dust from pulverized seashells; the lime in this dust, when chewed with coca leaves, releases the plant's narcotic effects. The crowned head of a hawk may have decorated a royal scepter or staff. Discovery of simpler, personal ornaments on Pizarro's first voyages along the Colombian coast lured him southward in quest of Inca wealth. In Ecuador, he came upon ceramic figures like those above; in Peru, he found delicate necklaces like those at far right—one crafted of gold and stone, the other of gold and shell.

sailed for southern Colombia and dropped Pizarro and his company to tramp in the mud again.

One vessel headed back to Panama for reinforcements; the other explored the coast. Near the Equator it overtook a giant raft of traders from Tumbes, the port city in Peru that Huayna Capac had embellished. Its cargo included woolens with animal designs woven in colors, clusters of beads and rubies, a balance for weighing gold, and mirrors of burnished silver. The Spaniards carried off some passengers to teach them to be interpreters.

Pizarro next pushed south to the populous Ecuadorean coast but halted reconnaissance when thousands of hostile Indians lined the shore at Esmeraldas, port of emeralds. He sent both vessels back to Panama for additional men. Lest the Governor of Panama abort the expedition, Pizarro and his discouraged men waited on the Isla del Gallo—Isle of the Rooster—opposite present-day Tumaco, Colombia.

The indignant Governor sent ships to bring everyone to Panama, but Pizarro refused to abandon the Isle of the Rooster. Tracing a line in the sand with his sword, he pointed south and said: "There lies toil, famine, nakedness, rainstorms, foresakenness, and death." Challenging his followers to risk Peru and riches or return to Panama and poverty, he stepped across the line. Thirteen joined him. Historians recorded the names of those who stayed with Pizarro on the island; to know that, I think, would have pleased them enormously. The rest returned to Panama. There Pizarro's partners, Almagro and the priest, tried to rekindle interest in the forlorn conquest of Peru.

Long curious to see the island so famous in New World history, I once navigated a seagoing dugout from Tumaco across 12 miles of riptides to visit the Isle of the Rooster, concealed in offshore mist. I had heard a rumor along the mangrove coast that the island's sole inhabitant was a sorceress.

Beaching the dugout, I walked toward a solitary dwelling perched on stilts in a coconut grove. Suddenly a white-haired black woman jumped out of a thicket and whacked me on the seat of my pants with the flat of a machete.

Dumbfounded, I ran a few steps and whirled. The old lady planted her bare feet and laughed.

"Now you'll never forget Jovita." She squinted at my camera. "So you've come to take pictures. Good. There's not much time left. I'm 84. I'm going to die next year."

I followed dutifully as Jovita led me on a tour, over black sand and white, past patterned driftwood, through wet jungle and abandoned coconut groves, and into secret caves. I asked if she were really a sorceress. She admitted a knack for cures.

"Until 1906," she told me, "there was a village here. Then a tidal wave swept it away." Jovita was one of the survivors.

She ran into the surf until the Pacific Ocean lapped at her skirt. "Here Pizarro landed!" She strode ashore, brandishing her machete, re-enacting her own version of the historic moment. She cried: "I take possession of this land in the name of the King of Spain!" Then with her blade she sliced a line in the sand, inviting me to join her in the conquest of the Incas. Before I could play my role by stepping across to volunteer, a wave washed the line away. Jovita laughed.

At her house, Jovita showed me two neatly folded flags, one Colombian and one Peruvian, that explained her awareness of island history. The flags had been hoisted over a bronze plaque to Pizarro, which had been set up near the beach during a binational visit of warships in 1965. Jovita, as the island's only resident, had been left in charge of the flags. She hid them to prevent theft by beachcombers, but kept a seaward watch, ready to run out and hoist the colors when the vessels returned. I wondered who would guard the flags if Jovita died at age 85, as she anticipated.

The tide had gone out. When I bent to launch my dugout, Jovita belted me on the rear again with the flat of her machete.

"Remember me!" She waved.

Pizarro and his faithful 13 companions had languished on this and another island for five months when a rescue caravel came over the horizon. Then Pizarro's fortunes rallied. Unencumbered by an army, he sailed not home but south across the Equator to Tumbes, where his floating castle dropped anchor in the Tumbes River. Several rafts steered out with loads of plantains, cocoa, corn, sweet potatoes, pineapples, and llamas—and the first Inca to greet Europeans, a noble with massive earplugs.

The noble supped with Pizarro, listened to talk in a strange tongue about supremacy of God and King, and returned to Tumbes with the gift of an iron hatchet. He surely sent a chasqui to Huayna Capac with news of the bearded men, the strangers who so perturbed the emperor in his final years.

Next day, a Spaniard and a Negro took ashore a rooster whose crowing delighted the natives. They came back with incredible reports of pleasure gardens, treasure, and offers of beautiful wives. Pizarro, skeptical, then sent a trusted companion, Pedro de Candía, a Greek artilleryman in polished armor. After demonstrating his thunder-speaking arquebus, Candía was shown temple artisans making imitation fruits and vegetables of gold and silver.

Francisco Pizarro: Exploration and Invasion
— 1524-1525
— 1526-1527
— 1531-1533

From 1524 to 1533, Pizarro probed the coast, found the Inca Empire, and took Cuzco.

"The Spaniards were nearly mad with joy," wrote the historian Prescott. But Pizarro still lamented the fate which had deprived him of his invasion force. In fact, according to Prescott, he was lucky: "Peru was not yet torn asunder . . . and might well have bid defiance to all the forces that Pizarro could muster."

"It was manifestly the work of Heaven," exclaimed another writer, a devout son of the Church, "that the natives of the country should have received him in so kind and loving a spirit, as best fitted to facilitate the conquest."

Pizarro's caravel quested on south, touching along the driest coast in the world in contrast to one of the rainiest where the voyage had begun. Though most of the civilized sites seemed to be abodes of the dead, with countless mummies preserved in sandy tombs and adobe temples, the Spaniards visited several irrigated

Churning surf scours a beach of black sand in northern Peru, uncovering tiny shellfish for hungry birds. Sailing south from Panama, Pizarro passed miles of wild coast, much of it unchanged even today. Broad wings spread, egrets (below) take flight at the Gulf of Guayaquil. At bottom, dense mangrove thickets fringe shoreline typical of southern Colombia and northern Ecuador. Pizarro cut through such tangled growth to explore inland.

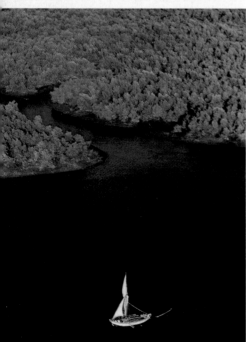

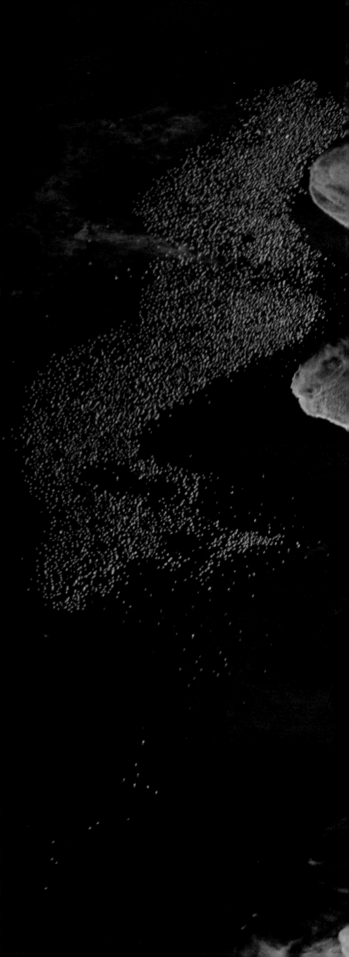

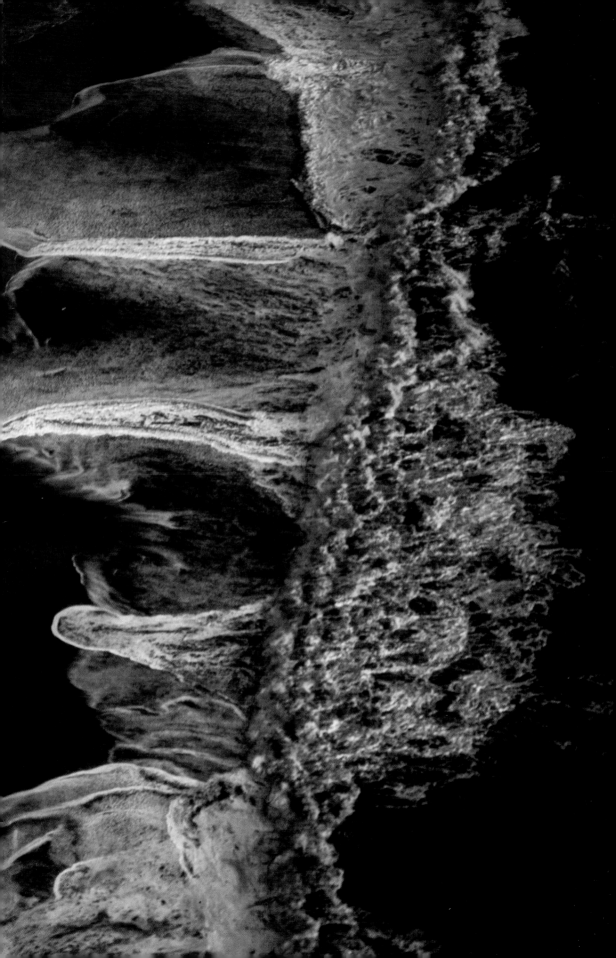

Overleaf: In the first meeting between Spaniards and Inca nobility, gift-laden rafts converge on Pizarro's caravel as it comes to anchor in the mouth of the Tumbes River. The flotilla bears fish, fruit, llamas—and an Inca noble wearing large golden earplugs. He will dine with the bearded Europeans, unaware that his host will overthrow the empire.

oases where Andean rivers trickled to the shore. Peaceful inhabitants entertained them and added to their collection of treasure, llamas, and intelligence on imperial Cuzco—which at first the conquistadors mistook for the name of the Son of the Sun.

They reached a fine harbor at latitude 9° south—site of present-day Chimbote—and then turned back. After stopping at Tumbes to drop off two Spaniards who wanted to stay, they sped to Panama with winds astern.

Pizarro's unexpected reappearance there in 1528 with "Peruvian sheep," Quechua-speaking natives, and golden trinkets failed to impress the Governor. He refused to back further folly in Peru. So Pizarro's partners sent the conquistador to Spain, which he had not seen in more than 20 years.

King Charles I *was* impressed by the gold, the llamas, and Pizarro's tales, especially his account of his performance on Isla del Gallo. The timely presence of Hernando Cortés at court reminded Charles how a scant 600 Spaniards had conquered Mexico and brought him treasure. The new wealth was most useful for Charles, since he was the Holy Roman Emperor as well as the King of Spain, and European hegemony kept him deeply in debt. To invest in the conquest of Peru cost him nothing but the granting of a few grandiose titles.

Pizarro received what every adventurous Spaniard longed for: authority to do what he wanted. And the stalwarts of Isla del Gallo became hidalgos, somebodies.

The Council of the Indies, which supervised Spain's interests in the New World, licensed Pizarro to raise 150 men in Spain and 100 more from the colonies, and bound him to sail within six months. The Council also enjoined him to protect the natives, assigning priests to see to their spiritual conversion while banning lawyers lest they stir up litigation.

Pizarro first made a pilgrimage to his birthplace, Trujillo, in Extremadura. There he enlisted his four half-brothers. But he had trouble raising funds and finding men; Seville was so stripped of manpower by emigration to the Indies that "the city was left almost to the women," observed the Venetian ambassador.

When Pizarro did arrive in Panama with his arrogant brothers and a sheaf of titles, his partner Almagro threatened to quit. Instead of an equal hand, Almagro found that Pizarro had dealt him only the piddling command of the fortress of Tumbes—the first of many affronts. Though embittered, Almagro finally agreed to

Verdant Cabo Corrientes emerges briefly from downpours that dump 300 inches of rain a year; Pizarro skirted the cape, a two-day sail from Panama, on his first expedition. On his next voyage, he reached a harbor ringed with dunes near the mouth of the Santa River in Peru— one of earth's driest regions. On his third expedition, Pizarro journeyed on this Inca coastal road before turning inland to confront Atahuallpa.

remain in Panama looking for volunteers. Then the so-called Governor and Captain General of Peru, Francisco Pizarro, embarked with 180 men and 37 horses in three small Panama-built caravels. He sailed as the year 1531 began, on his third and last chance to make the Inca Empire his own.

Pizarro needed more than 180 men for the invasion. Perhaps for that reason he chose to land in northern Ecuador, beyond Inca reach. While ships paced him offshore, he slogged south through a mangrove morass and fell upon a peaceful hamlet, sacking it. Luckily for his ambitions, it proved rich in treasure—though soldiers smashed a fortune in emeralds by testing their hardness with a hammer. Pizarro sent the loot to Panama to entice recruits and pay for more horses and supplies.

They reached him in driblets. A royal treasurer and inspector came from Spain; thirty men arrived under Sebastián de Benalcázar, who had voyaged with Columbus in 1498 and would later found many great South American cities. Pizarro fumed and waited for reinforcements all through 1531; he was unmolested by highlanders, for civil war had snapped the bonds of the Inca Empire.

In the withering heat at the Equator, some of his men died of ugly ulcers; others despaired. But not until they ran afoul of the islanders of Puná—those shrewd cannibals who had drowned Huayna Capac's expeditionaries in the gulf—did the Spaniards have to fight for their lives. Though several were killed and a javelin pierced Hernando Pizarro's leg, the chronicles report that Saint Michael and his legions appeared in the sky and saved the day.

At last another Extremaduran, Hernando de Soto, arrived with 100 men from Nicaragua and dozens of horses. The Spaniards quickly forsook Puná and rafted across the Gulf of Guayaquil to Tumbes, where they had received a lavish welcome five years earlier. To Pizarro's dismay, they found Tumbes demolished by the civil war that rent the empire. There was no trace of the two comrades who had chosen to stay there.

For fear that his men might lose heart, Pizarro pressed south. On long desert marches and during lengthy stays in well-irrigated oases, he picked up Indian auxiliaries and increasing information about the Inca Empire. He founded a settlement—later relocated and grown into today's city of Piura—and named it San Miguel de Piura in honor of the archangel.

Twenty months after he had left Panama, the main body of reinforcements he expected under Almagro still had not arrived. Troops became restive. Pizarro lost patience. Nearly eight years had passed since he first set out for Peru. He was approaching 60, twice the average longevity of men in his times.

Learning that the Inca Atahuallpa awaited in the highlands, Pizarro left San Miguel to the colonists, the sick, the Crown bureaucrats, and the faint of heart. On September 24, 1532, with little but their lives to lose and an empire to gain, he and his 167 followers struck out for Cajamarca.

Precipitous trail leads Spaniards into the Andes toward Atahuallpa's camp at Cajamarca. Cavalrymen pulled their mounts step by step in the cold, thin air. All 168 men and 62 horses survived the perilous trip.

CHAPTER SEVEN

GOLD LLAMA FOUND IN A TOMB NEAR LAKE
TITICACA, MUSEUM AND INSTITUTE OF ARCHEOLOGY,
UNIVERSITY OF SAN ANTONIO ABAD, CUZCO

The

APPROACHING CAJAMARCA from the western mountains, the invaders kept to high ground to avoid ambush. On the morning of November 15, 1532, Francisco Pizarro reined his horse upon sighting a vast blanket of mist two thousand feet below. Scalding overflow from hot springs—the Inca's Bath—wended through lush meadows and filled the valley of Cajamarca with vapor by night. When the sun rose high, it lifted the mist from a scene as fantastic as any in the knight-errantry book of *Amadís*.

A town glinted like gold as sunbeams played on yellow thatch. Beyond, green farmland reached across a gentle vale. On the far slope, surrounding columns of vapor that marked the hot springs, spread a pageant that caused many a Spaniard to cross himself and breathe a few Hail Mary's.

"The Indians' camp looked like a very beautiful city," scribbled a rough soldier who wanted his children to remember his strange adventure. "So many were the tents that we were filled with fright. We never thought the Indians could occupy such a proud position, nor so many tents, so well set up. . . . It filled all us Spaniards with confusion and fear. But we dared not show it, much less turn back, for if they sensed the least weakness in us, the very Indians we brought with us would have killed us. So with a show of good spirits, after having thoroughly surveyed the town and tents . . . we descended into the valley below and entered the town of Cajamarca."

In describing one of the most dramatic confrontations in history, later storytellers ignored a fact which the soldier-eyewitness had let slip: Pizarro and his band were not alone. Enough Indians accompanied the Spaniards that they feared annihilation by their own auxiliaries. Indian collaboration would help explain Pizarro's lunatic nerve in pitting 168 Spaniards against anywhere from 30,000 to 80,000 Inca warriors. He would have been hewing to the example of Cortés in Mexico who counted on local dissidents for support. Had Pizarro invaded before or after the civil war he might have found no auxiliaries and been quickly vanquished.

Pizarro followed a route inland so steep at times that his cavalry had to dismount and climb by hand and foot. After years in hot and humid lowlands, men grew faint and nauseated in

Eclipse of the Sun

*Steaming waters from hot springs that fill the Inca's Bath flow past a
highland girl at Cajamarca, Peru. On nearby slopes, Atahuallpa made
his headquarters while he rested his army and awaited the Spaniards.*

Riding in a shawl sling, a baby—just christened in Cajamarca—peeks over the shoulder of her mother, who wears traditional clothing of that region. In a broad valley, Cajamarca (below) glows with light. On the night of November 15, 1532, flickering campfires of thousands of Inca warriors blazed on the hillsides, appearing "like a starry sky" to one of Pizarro's sentries. The 168 Spaniards had arrived at a ridge above Cajamarca earlier that day and sighted the Inca camp. Perceiving no hostile actions, they descended into the city and found it evacuated. Occupying the central plaza, the Spaniards spent a sleepless night. Even Pizarro stood watch as he tensely anticipated a confrontation with Atahuallpa, thirteenth Inca, commander of an overwhelming army, and ruler of an empire about which the conquistador knew little.

rarefied air at elevations up to 11,000 feet. Luckily for them, the passes in northern Peru are among the lowest in the Andes.

Luckier still, they marched without opposition from the Inca Atahuallpa; rather, he sent observers with gifts. The Spaniards found the town of Cajamarca evacuated—by order of Atahuallpa, who waited at the hot springs nearly four miles away. Though perplexed by Inca inaction, Pizarro quickly dispatched 20 riders under Hernando de Soto to offer his services in arms to the Inca and invite him to visit next day. Hernando Pizarro followed later with 20 more horsemen. Several of these steel-nerved envoys penned eyewitness accounts.

De Soto left his men at the last stream crossing and rode into the camp through a corridor of halberdiers. The Spaniard carried an Indian interpreter behind him on his horse. Atahuallpa awaited in the company of wives and courtiers outside his red-walled pleasure house, where, says a chronicler, "two pipes of water, one hot and one cold, entered the bathing pool." Small wonder that many conquistadors thought of Incas as "Moors": Bathing was a Muslim custom condemned in Spain. Too, at the confrontation between the Spaniard and the Inca, Atahuallpa "was seated on a small stool, very low to the ground, as Turks and Moors are accustomed to sit."

De Soto delivered a speech from horseback. Atahuallpa did not lift his eyes, nonplussing the bold cavalier. The awkwardness ended when Hernando Pizarro arrived and caught the Inca's attention by identifying himself as brother of the Governor—*El Gobernador*—the title awarded by the Spanish Crown which distinguished Francisco from the other Pizarro brothers.

Atahuallpa's intense curiosity about the bearded men now overcame his regal reserve. He listened to badly interpreted bombast and accepted the invitation to visit the Governor next day. The Inca asked the Spaniards to dismount. They declined, but drank ceremonial chicha from golden flagons despite their fear of poisoning. Before departing, the audacious De Soto charged up to Atahuallpa and reined back his steed. The Inca sat impassively on the royal stool. Some of the warriors flinched.

That night Atahuallpa had the soldiers who had shown alarm executed. He planned a show of might next day, and designated a force under cruel General Rumiñahui—"Eye of Stone"—to cut off the invaders' escape route to the coast in the event they fled.

To an apprehensive Spanish sentry, Inca campfires on the far hillside seemed "like a starry sky . . . a menacing thing. . . ." Soldiers whetted swords and prayed, feeling more like crusaders about to be martyred than conquerors. On his rounds, the Governor said: "Make fortresses of your hearts for you have no other."

"All were full of fear," recalled the sentry, "for we were so few and so deep in the land where we could not be reinforced. . . ." The Spaniards gambled on an extremely risky recourse: the capture of the king. They would hide in public buildings—with doorways high enough for horse and rider—that opened on a triangular walled plaza with an entrance at its apex. They hoped to entice the Inca into their midst and kidnap him.

On Saturday, November 16, 1532, the Inca delayed his social

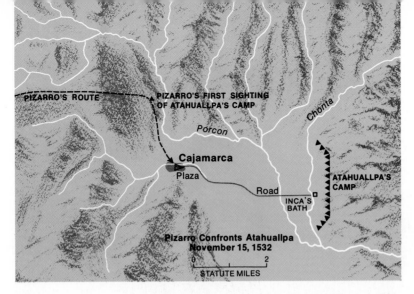

Rimmed by mountains, Cajamarca's valley spreads almost four miles between town and Inca camp. As Atahuallpa relaxed at his bath, the Spaniards, greatly outnumbered, devised a strategy to capture him.

call until sundown, relying on information that horses were useless after dark, and bemused by reports that the bearded men were hiding in abject fear. In fact, as the meadows filled with Inca soldiers, "many Spaniards wet their pants from terror without noticing it," recorded Pedro Pizarro, cousin of the Governor.

Atahuallpa actually had started for Cajamarca in early afternoon, proceeding slowly and with pomp. His escort wore colorful livery, and his nobles displayed gold and silver disks on their foreheads. Half a mile from town, the Inca suddenly halted his splendid procession and began to pitch camp for the night.

This dismayed the nervous Spaniards. In desperation, the Governor sent one last envoy to urge the Inca onward. Atahuallpa resumed the march, so sure of his invulnerability that his escort went unarmed. His experienced generals Quisquis and Chalcuchima might have counseled caution. But they were campaigning in the Cuzco area, where Chalcuchima had recently captured Emperor Huascar, pulling him from his litter.

The sun of the Incas was sinking in the west, its long rays shining in the faces of the marchers and "making their gold and silver medallions blaze strangely," the Governor's cousin wrote. Few Spaniards could see what was going on. They waited behind dark doorways, silent but for the occasional uneasy jingle of cascabels on horses' trappings.

The Inca was preceded by hundreds of singers and dancers, whose triumphant cries, said one conqueror, "sounded like the songs of hell." Atahuallpa entered the plaza on a golden litter bedecked with parrot feathers. Several great lords and chieftains rode litters and hammocks behind him. Five or six thousand nobles and soldiers squeezed into the plaza.

When no bearded ones appeared, Atahuallpa demanded, "Where are they?"

At this, the Dominican friar Vicente de Valverde came forward in white cassock and black hood, with cross and prayer book

in hand. He harangued Atahuallpa with his version of the extraordinary Requirement that Spaniards had to make known to natives before drawing their swords. This document reflected the moral concern in Spain about the rights and wrongs of New World conquest. Friar Valverde's wordy farrago began with a Biblical history of the world and described the Holy Trinity, the Crucifixion and Resurrection of Jesus, papal history, and the Pope's award of the Indies to Spain. It obliged the listener to recognize Church, Pope, and the King, lest death and losses from attack be "your fault."

The interpreter got the ultimatum's point across, and it outraged the Inca. Bend to another monarch? Kneel to another God, one crucified by His own people? What oracle uttered such sacrilege to the Son of the Sun?

Friar Valverde handed up the prayer book to the Inca, saying, "it speaks the truth."

Atahuallpa picked at the clasp, striking away the monk's arm when he reached to help. The breviary fell open. It was a small huaca at best, a minor god of thin squared leaves. It did not speak to Atahuallpa. He glowered and threw it down.

Friar Valverde recovered it and scuttled away, calling on God.

The Inca rose and pointed to the sun, now about to set. "My God still lives in the heavens, and looks down on his children." His minions stood silently steadfast.

In that instant a blast of bugles startled them. Guns thundered. A Spanish war cry echoed from trapezoidal doorways: *"Santiago! Y a ellos!*—Saint James! And at them!"

Silver-shirted monsters charged out of the shadows. Hooves rang on flagstones, then thudded into Indian flesh. Jangling breastplate bells underscored screams as heavy lances tilted at bodies too tightly packed to flee. Toledo blades thrust, slashed, and spattered blood.

Terror swept the courtyard. Indians cowered as if supernatural forces had descended with the swift tropical night. The Governor, on foot, wearing quilted cotton armor, cut his way with sword and dagger toward Atahuallpa. When steel severed the hands of the Inca's litter bearers, they sustained the royal platform with their shoulders. As they fell, other bearers replaced them. Then, for the second time that year, a golden litter was profaned and a Son of the Sun fell to earth. The Governor was cut on the hand when he parried a soldier's dagger thrust at Atahuallpa. Spaniards hurried the Inca into a nearby building for safekeeping.

Lancers galloped over dying Indians and pursued survivors into the night. The horsemen mercilessly rode down fleeing warriors on the plain until bugles recalled them. Eyewitnesses estimated the Indian dead at two to eight thousand; Atahuallpa said seven thousand. Incredibly, no Spaniard died and the Governor's cut hand was the only wound reported.

Jagged rock pillars line a crest of the Continental Divide in central Peru. Holding Atahuallpa in Cajamarca, Pizarro sent two expeditions through this wilderness—one to Cuzco, the other to the coast—to speed delivery of ransom. Bearers and llamas brought back such treasure that the "road seemed paved with gold," one chronicler wrote.

149

The ferocity of the Spaniards subsided almost as suddenly as it had risen. To the Inca's astonishment, the Governor treated him courteously and they supped together that night. Atahuallpa admitted having intended to sacrifice some Spaniards to the Sun and to castrate others as guards for his many wives. He also planned to breed the horses, which he greatly admired.

From then on, the Governor permitted subjects to visit Atahuallpa and encouraged him to rule from his prison. Female attendants held food to his mouth and ceremonially burned everything that he discarded. They dressed the Inca immaculately. He showed the Governor's wide-eyed cousin a robe woven of bat fur. Atahuallpa maintained his air of dignity with the Spaniards and the customary aloofness from his subjects. Great chiefs from distant provinces still trembled in his presence.

But the sad truth was that the Inca Empire had fallen into disarray in the final months of 1532, less than a century after Pachacuti first stormed out of Cuzco bent on conquest. In Cuzco itself, as a devastating civil war ended, Emperor Huascar was the captive of insurgents serving his victorious half-brother Atahuallpa, who soon had him executed. And while Atahuallpa still controlled the Four Quarters of the World, he exercised his rule from confinement in Cajamarca, a two weeks' relay by chasquis from the capital. Yet his Spanish captors had barely penetrated the empire, knew little of its size and organization, and dared not march farther without reinforcements. The invaders, in turn, were vassals of a king so far away that communication with him required a journey to the Pacific Coast, a voyage to Panama, transit of the Isthmus, passage of the Atlantic to Europe, and overland travel.

Not until long after the slaughter at Cajamarca did Charles I see his share of Atahuallpa's ransom, history's greatest for a king. To win freedom, Atahuallpa offered to fill a 17-by-22-foot room once with gold, as high as he could reach, and twice with silver.

Historian Rodolfo Ravines, director of Cajamarca's archeological museum, showed Sue and me his model of the triangular plaza. He took us to the only Inca structure left in town, which he believes to be the stone-walled ransom room. A red line now marks the level which the pile of treasure was supposed to have reached. Although Atahuallpa had promised delivery within two months, treasure had to be taken from the empire's holy places. Priests were evidently slow to release images of gold and silver to free the lord who had just overthrown their emperor.

To speed the flow of gold, Hernando Pizarro—who had been patrolling south of Cajamarca—rode on to distant Pachacamac in January, 1533. During an audacious journey through rain-lashed highlands recently subjugated by Atahuallpa, he visited 18 towns and reached the desert coast unmolested. At Pachacamac, the inner sanctum of one of the most revered shrines in the realm turned out to be a filthy chamber. The Spaniards destroyed it.

Hernando had an old priest tortured but found less treasure than he expected in weeks of search. He returned with a different prize: Chalcuchima, greatest of Atahuallpa's generals, who until then had been in position to exterminate every Spaniard in Peru.

Chalcuchima had made the mistake of his life. "Sweet-talked"

Casting bullion, Indians drop artwork into a crucible at Cajamarca. Fires blazed for a month, melting down 24 tons of gold and silver.

—as a chronicler wrote—by Hernando Pizarro, he had voluntarily left his huge army at Jauja, in central Peru, to accompany the conquistador to Cajamarca.

His mounts outfitted with silver horseshoes forged by Indian artisans, Hernando crossed lofty snowfields and swaying suspension bridges as he returned by the main highway, visiting 22 towns. Along the way, General Chalcuchima, who rode a litter and was treated with the reverence due an Inca, cheerfully described his civil war victories to his new European friend. Yet not long after reaching Cajamarca, the General was carried to Hernando Pizarro's lodgings "with his legs and arms burned and his tendons shriveled" from torture by De Soto to make him reveal gold hoards —about which he knew nothing. Whether from compassion or self-interest, Hernando dressed Chalcuchima's wounds.

Since Cuzco's gold was slow to come, the Governor commended to God three expendable soldiers and dispatched them toward the Inca capital. Native runners carried them in hammocks. A Negro accompanying the soldiers halted in Jauja while the others went on to pillage Cuzco's Temple of the Sun. With the surly

Cloud-parting summits dominate the highlands of central Peru, a harsh land crossed by the force of about 200 men and 100 horses that Pizarro led from Cajamarca to Cuzco. On a plateau amid these mountains, the invaders encountered Inca resistance — the first since landing in Peru 17 months earlier. Inca foot soldiers, however, proved no match for Spaniards mounted on swift horses, and the Indians scattered. The horsemen pursued, overtaking and spearing the Indians in their flight. Even today, many South Americans rely on horses, first introduced by the conquistadors; at sunup, a lone rider dressed in poncho and fedora heads for market along the Peruvian altiplano northwest of Cuzco.

consent of Quisquis, general of Atahuallpa's occupation army, they pried 700 plates of gold from the temple frieze. As related by historian John Hemming, they found an old woman who wore a golden mask; she fanned flies from two mummified Incas. She ordered them to remove their boots before entering a sanctuary. They complied meekly, and then "stole many rich objects" from the mummies. Citizens of Cuzco were reluctant to assist in the desecration of the temple. Their hopes waned—how could these bearded ones be the "Viracochas" sent by the supreme being Viracocha to save the captive populace from Atahuallpa?

Within five months, the first Europeans to visit imperial Cuzco returned to Cajamarca with 285 loads of loot borne by Indians and llamas. From Jauja, the Negro brought 107 loads of gold and seven of silver. By mid-1533 more than 24 tons of exquisite treasure had been delivered: idols and chalices, necklaces and nuggets, dismantled altars and fountains. Spanish bookkeepers, in page after page, itemized such objects: a golden stalk of corn, 38 gold vessels 50 to 75 pounds, and a solid gold image the size of a young boy. Though only a fraction of the plunder awaiting the conquistadors, Atahuallpa's ransom, when reduced to bullion, was worth at least 30 million dollars at 1975's values for gold and silver.

Nine blazing fires reduced priceless creations to lumps of gleaming metal. Each soldier's share was 45 pounds of gold and 90 of silver. Riders received two shares each, De Soto four, Hernando Pizarro seven, and the Governor 13 shares as well as Atahuallpa's 200-pound golden litter.

The day before Easter, 1533, the Governor's partner, Diego de Almagro, arrived with horses and men that nearly doubled the invasion force. As the newcomers received only a token share of Atahuallpa's ransom, they clamored to be done with him and get on to plunder Cuzco, a thousand road miles away.

When the ransom room was empty, Atahuallpa was not freed nor could he escape his captors. He knew that his life was running out because a comet—*tapiya qoylyor,* ill-omened star—had passed over. Then two conquistadors who might have defended him departed. Hernando Pizarro left for Spain with many magnificent objects saved from melting as part of the King's share. And Hernando de Soto went to investigate a rumor that Atahuallpa had ordered an attack by Rumiñahui, the general who had left Cajamarca the night of Pizarro's victory. The rumor proved false; Rumiñahui had led his troops north to Ecuador.

Without these leaders to argue his claim on life, Atahuallpa was sentenced to die. The charges against him included murdering Huascar and, incredibly, treason against the strangers within his own realm. To avoid the horror of being burned at the stake as an infidel and thus being deprived of mummification and afterlife, Atahuallpa accepted baptism. He took his conqueror's Christian name, Francisco. Friar Valverde, whose prayer book Atahuallpa had thrown down eight months earlier, performed the rites.

Then, in the great triangular plaza of Cajamarca, the Spaniards garroted Francisco Atahuallpa, thirteenth Inca.

News of the execution caught up with Hernando Pizarro in Panama and traveled on the same treasure galleon with him to

Spain. Charles I received Hernando grandly. But even before seeing the Inca treasures, he ordered them minted into coin. Then he wrote to the Governor of Peru: ". . . we have been displeased by the death of Atahuallpa, since he was a monarch. . . ." In the view of royalty, Francisco Pizarro had committed regicide.

He also had created anarchy by decapitating the empire. The clockwork of Inca government — ticking throughout the civil war — ran down. At Cajamarca, during the eight stagnant months, Spaniards and Incas raided warehouses and consumed thousands of llamas — a pattern that was to continue.

With the arrival of Almagro, the time had come to strike into the heart of the empire. The Governor and his men left Cajamarca on August 11, 1533, with Almagro, De Soto, captive General Chalcuchima, and a puppet Inca, Tupa Huallpa. They marched halfway to Cuzco without conflict. The stone-stepped Inca highway led past Peru's most spectacular snowcapped ranges and onto an undulating upland more than two miles high. Then, near Jauja, they clashed with the army of occupation once commanded by General Chalcuchima. The northern Incas were the first to fight Francisco Pizarro since his landing in Tumbes, Peru, 17 months earlier.

The Spaniards charged aggressively and proved again that a small band of cavalry could scatter an entire Inca army on the plain — though not in the mountains, they would soon learn.

Welcoming the Spaniards to the city of Jauja, Huanca tribesmen there revealed widespread resentment of Inca despotism. The Governor capitalized on it. He founded at Jauja the first Christian capital of Peru, and assigned his sick and injured soldiers to guard accumulated booty. The rest of his men made out their wills.

De Soto and 70 cavalrymen spurred ahead without tents or baggage, aiming to capture suspension bridges along the 500-mile route to Cuzco. Almagro and the Governor followed with the remaining force of horsemen and foot

Andean girl cradles her puppy. Like most highlanders today, she has a mix of Indian and Spanish blood.

soldiers. Chalcuchima, under guard, accompanied them. He was suspected of having poisoned Tupa Huallpa, who had died unexpectedly in Jauja.

The vanguard found that Quito armies, retreating toward Cuzco, had burned some bridges. But Spanish luck held. It was November, and the summer rains must have been late, for the water was low. De Soto's cavalry descended into the Apurimac gorge and swam the great river without loss.

Part way out of the gorge, while horses panted from the elevation and the steep climb, the Spaniards encountered a storm of slingstones, and thousands of painted warriors screamed down the slope. De Soto sounded the charge — in vain. Exhausted steeds could not answer the spur. Indians grabbed the horses' tails. Others swung star-headed maces. The skulls of five Spaniards

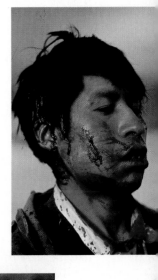

Cracking his whip and shouting "wanuchiy! —kill," a horseman charges toward the author during a ritual war held yearly on a Peruvian mountaintop above the Apurimac River near Cuzco. Indians of neighboring Chumbivilcas and Canas provinces become enemies for a day, vying to capture maidens for trial marriage. With deadly accuracy, a Canas slingman (below) hurls stones the size of golf balls. Incas used such weapons in imperial conquest and in defense against the Spaniards. After a morning of conflict, the combatants withdraw to hilltop bases, eat a picnic lunch served by matrons and their unwed daughters, and rekindle their enthusiasm for battle with ritual drinking. Women (below, left) join hands on a hill above the field to wail a three-note Inca chant showing concern for the wounded. At dusk, the conflict ends. Both sides, friends again, dress their wounds with coca-leaf poultices. A young Chumbivilcan (right) suffered severe head wounds and later died—one of two fatalities. The Incas held such mock battles between neighbors at the end of each year.

were shattered before the conquistadors rallied to a hillock with 11 men and 14 horses wounded. Two of the dead were very rich men. They had been provident to make out their wills.

Inca warriors jeered and brandished strange insignia on their lances: severed horses' heads and tails. Darkness fell. De Soto's cavalry tensed, expecting attack. Past midnight a miraculous sound floated up from the gorge: the call of a bugle. Fearing for De Soto, Pizarro had dispatched Almagro and 30 horsemen. The joint force charged at daybreak; the Indians faded into the mist.

Even today, slingmen wage mortal combat with cavalrymen on Apurimac mountainsides. Upriver from the site of De Soto's brush with death, I once found myself a foot soldier amid rampaging riders in a ritual war fought yearly since Inca times. It happened when Sue and I called on a peasant friend, Luis Choqueneira, whose stone hut perched at 13,000 feet on the edge of the upper Apurimac gorge. Luis and his scattered neighbors of Canas Province stem from ancestors who had resisted Pachacuti.

"We're tough," boasted Luis. "We fight with bolas like this." He whirled a cord with three weights attached and sent it spinning. It tangled in the legs and curled-up tail of a yellow-eyed dog, which tumbled to the ground, yipping. "Some of us will get killed trying to capture the enemy's girls."

"The enemy? Who's the enemy?"

"Well, our friends of Chumbivilcas Province become enemies for a day. When they're short of men, we lend them some of ours."

In a flurry of midsummer snow next morning we climbed 15,590-foot Tocto, a summit 900 feet higher than Switzerland's Matterhorn. There we joined hundreds of picnicking Indians who wore embroidered woolens and hats bedecked with fresh flowers. Single women joined hands and circled, cooing mournful sounds like the Inca dirges described by chronicler priests.

Canas slingmen gathered stones the size of golf balls; riders galloped over rocks and crocuses, shouting to summon their nerve and pausing only to gulp straight cane alcohol. Chumbivilcan cavalry pranced atop a hill a mile away, silhouetted against the murky sky. Sue and I wished that we could see their maidens dancing; in Inca times Chumbivilcans danced for the court to pay their labor tax. Now they were our enemy.

Suddenly the Tocto war was on—our slingmen were storming the far hill. I chased after them with my camera. Slings cracked like whips. Rocks whooshed with terrifying speed and range. There were no communications, no bugle calls to rally cavalry. I couldn't tell hooting friend from jeering foe.

A riderless stallion galloped by. Luis tugged me to haven behind a boulder, warning, "Get back to Tocto summit!" I didn't heed him, but followed our cavalry up the hill. Chumbivilcan matrons fled screaming from the crest into the next valley, though

Burgeoning tassels of European wheat ripen on a plain above the Urubamba River. From across the Atlantic, Spanish colonists brought new plants and animals to South America. Sheep, like llamas, soon grazed sparse highlands, supplying meat and wool. Weathered hands hold kernels of barley, a grain that grows at higher altitudes than corn.

unwed daughters dawdled—hoping to be captured by doughty Canas bachelors. Then the enemy counterattacked, and I learned all too vividly how the Inca foot soldier must have felt when run down by Spanish knights.

A Chumbivilcan cavalry charge trapped me in the open valley. Riders thundered down the slopes, their whips resounding like rifle shots. I ran for my life. A hail of Canas slingstones toppled one assailant. Others veered as I dived behind a large boulder. I felt as helpless as if caught by an avalanche.

That evening, at Luis's hut, his wife applied a coca-leaf poultice to an ugly bruise on his temple. Luis calmly reported, "Only two dead. Chumbivilcans."

We had first met Luis while looking for the remnant of a *keshwa chaca*—straw bridge—over the Apurimac. From the air, I had once spotted a suspension span at a place unmentioned in the chronicles or by modern explorers. One day, after long questioning and search, we found it, abandoned but still hanging! Gleaming like Inca gold, the keshwa chaca swayed 60 feet above the river. We clawed 300 feet down a precipice to reach it.

Then a voice cautioned, "Don't cross! The bridge is dying!" It was Luis Choqueneira who warned us. He said, "I'm one of the *chaca camayocs*—keepers of the bridge. We're going to rebuild it, just as Tupa Inca ordered our ancestors to do every year. Come back in January if you want to see."

We did. A week after the Tocto war, hundreds of Canas and Chumbivilcas Indians—no longer enemies, and wearing fresh flowers in their hats—carried to the bridge site about 22,000 feet of hand-spun rope, finger-thick. Men twisted and braided the rope into six big cables. Children pounded sheaves of *coyo,* a tough bunchgrass, to make it pliable. From it, women spun more cordage.

Next day, work narrowed to a hundred members of Luis's community, responsible since empire days for actually hanging the bridge. Boys floated messenger lines across the river. Men then hauled the big cables across, tightening and securing them by sheer muscle power to horizontal stone bollards anchored in bedrock. Snug lashings caged the sides, from hand ropes to foot cables, so that no one might fall. On the last day three old chaca camayocs wove a footing of twigs. And that was all. It had taken 14 hours of work to rebuild the 100-foot-long bridge completely. All the while, offerings of coca leaves and sequin-spangled ears of corn smoldered by the foundations.

They honored Sue and me by letting us cross first. We stepped out over a torrent swollen with summer rain. Ritual smoke wreathed the faces of the men of Canas, battered by the Tocto war. They cheered us on. Some tossed their hats into the air, scattering the little bouquets. Those tough and wonderful Indians made Sue and me—alone in their midst—feel as if we had been transported back to the days when the sun of the Incas stood at zenith.

Downriver, some 440 years earlier, the conquistador who

Indian communities join each January to rebuild the last Inca bridge spanning the Apurimac River. Women spin bunchgrass for siding while men align thick cables that form the base and handrails of the bridge.

Torrential waters of the Apurimac River swirl below the keshwa chaca — straw bridge — as volunteer workers anchor the new span to rock and begin to cage the sides. Before unrolling a footing of twigs, a Canas Indian (below) tests the bridge; villagers construct it using more than 22,000 feet of rope spun from coyo — stalks of tubular grass hammered flat. The finished span can support dozens of people, but deteriorates within a year. Conquering Incas built such rope bridges to enable their vast armies to cross rivers during all seasons. They required local people to maintain and rebuild the bridges — important links in the empire's communication and transportation systems.

eclipsed that sun had forded the Apurimac with his 10 horsemen and 20 foot soldiers. The Governor caught up with his comrades, Almagro and De Soto, and they rode on to Xaquixaguana, where the causeway crosses the quagmire near Cuzco. There, they set fire to General Chalcuchima on suspicion of provoking Quito army resistance. The general died at the stake calling on Viracocha, though Friar Valverde tried to convert him to Christianity.

Pizarro still needed an Inca to run the country and command allegiance of the natives, and was delighted when a young prince —who had escaped Atahuallpa's Quito assassins—walked into the Spanish camp. He was Manco Inca, a son of Huayna Capac, and next in line for the royal fringe. Then, outside Cuzco, defending Inca troops rallied. Overcoming them, the Spaniards rode into the Inca capital on November 15, 1533, a year to the day after confronting Atahuallpa at Cajamarca.

Townspeople welcomed the invaders as liberating Viracochas, and Spanish leaders moved into Inca palaces. The Governor chose that of Pachacuti. Many took mistresses of royal blood. The Requirement was proclaimed to Cuzco's citizens. Though Pizarro, fearing uprising, had cautioned against abuse, conquistadors looted the city. His inspectors recorded the booty—more bounteous than that of Cajamarca—in 90 pages of legal documents. Eyewitnesses expressed amazement at warehouses filled with food, sandals, wool, copper, weapons, and shiny bird feathers for decorating garments. Manco's coronation as fifteenth Inca set in motion a riotous thirty-day festival. Parades of mummified Incas and llama sacrifices recalled the great days of empire.

Spaniards and Inca warriors campaigned side by side. When Quisquis's army attacked the Spanish garrison at Jauja, where plundered gold was stored, beleaguered Inca allies defended it. Presently, Manco Inca, with Indian troops led by Spanish cavalry, stormed out from Cuzco. He bridged mountain torrents and pursued Quisquis's hated northern armies halfway back to Ecuador.

By then, news from Peru had swept the Indies and Spain, and the gold rush was on. The King of Spain decreed, to no avail, that only merchants or men with wives should book for Peru. To stop exodus from Puerto Rico, its Governor even cut off settlers' feet.

The Governor of Guatemala, Pedro de Alvarado, took a different approach. He sailed in 12 small vessels with 500 Spaniards— 100 crossbowmen, 119 cavalrymen, and 281 foot soldiers—and 4,000 Guatemalan Indians who never saw home again.

Alvarado's proud and cruel army slowly destroyed both itself and local populaces, floundering in Ecuador's muggy western jungle and then freezing in snowbound passes. When Alvarado eventually reached the highway leading to Quito, he knew that he was too late: He sighted hoofprints left by the army of Pizarro's lieutenant, Sebastián de Benalcázar.

Benalcázar had been convoying Cajamarca gold to San Miguel de Piura. That seaport, south of Tumbes, now swarmed with

Devouring the sunset, threatening storm clouds gather over Bolivia's Lake Poopó. In Cuzco, two old Indians pass the time before La Compañía church, built on ruins of the palace of Emperor Huayna Capac.

adventurers lusting for combat and treasure. Learning of Alvarado's landing to the north, Benalcázar rushed with 200 men and 62 horses to beat him to Quito, the Inca Empire's northern capital.

In the mountains east of Guayaquil, the Spaniards marched directly into the midst of the northern Inca army. Perhaps 50,000 strong, it fought under Rumiñahui—the general who had moved north from Cajamarca.

This major battle cost the Incas 4,000 slain, and also badly bloodied Benalcázar's men, weakened by the 14,000-foot elevation. A renegade Indian showed the trapped Spaniards an escape route. They slipped away by night, a poet wrote, "as horizons grew sad and light vanished behind them, a thousand fires in the Spanish camp making a show of preparing their food."

Skirmishes strewed corpses all the way to Quito, and Rumiñahui put that city to the torch before Benalcázar got there. Spaniards finally scattered the Ecuadorean warriors and captured Rumiñahui. In vain they tortured him to locate hidden treasure. The Inca gold of Ecuador, if it indeed ever existed, has never been found.

Scorched earth also marked the 1,000-mile retreat of General Quisquis from Cuzco toward Quito. When his war-weary soldiers arrived to find Spaniards holding their Ecuadorean homeland, they murdered Quisquis and went to sow their fields.

With Ecuador subdued, Governor Pizarro journeyed to the coast in January 1535 to found a new capital, now called Lima. His partner Almagro set out from Cuzco in July to explore the southern half of the Inca Empire. He led 570 Spaniards and 12,000 Indians commanded by Paullu Inca, a son of Huayna Capac. Almagro had been named Governor of vague territory south of Cuzco—no maps existed—and he hoped that his "Land of Chile" glittered with gold. Had Almagro consulted quipu-keepers at Inca archives beforehand, he might have learned that his share of the Four Quarters of the World consisted largely of sand, some of the driest desert on earth.

De Soto departed for Spain. Other knights set out on expeditions. Juan and Gonzalo Pizarro, the Governor's brothers, were left to mind Cuzco's skeleton garrison. They badgered Manco Inca to reveal hidden gold, and molested his women. Manco escaped. Captured and brought back under heavy guard, he was reviled and befouled. Compounding his misery, priests and nobles brought him word of Spanish abuses throughout the land.

When Hernando Pizarro returned from Spain and took command of Cuzco, he befriended Manco and restored his freedom and dignity. But Manco had had enough of Spanish largess. The Viracochas, far from being liberators, were enslaving his people.

That vein of nobility which distinguished his forebears quickened in Manco Inca. He conspired with the high priest Villac Umu to raise an army and drive the Viracochas back into the sea whence they came. He made his move on Wednesday of Holy Week in 1536.

Desolate tract of sand and rock stretches to the horizon in Chile. Diego de Almagro, Pizarro's lieutenant, explored this southern part of the Inca Empire; finding no cities of gold, he returned to claim Cuzco for his own, but found it surrounded by an imposing army of Inca warriors.

CHAPTER EIGHT

CEREMONIAL SILVER BOWL WEIGHING ABOUT TWO
POUNDS. MUSEUM AND INSTITUTE OF ARCHEOLOGY,
UNIVERSITY OF SAN ANTONIO ABAD, CUZCO.

The Lost

MANCO, FIFTEENTH INCA, had been giving Hernando Pizarro occasional pieces of golden treasure to keep his trust. Now, behind the conquistador's back, Manco dispatched messengers with orders for large plantings of crops, gathering of weapons, and mobilization of troops throughout the Four Quarters of the World. Manco and his counselor, the high priest Villac Umu, somehow guarded their war plans from Indian collaborators who infested the realm.

Until Easter of 1536 every stroke of luck—or miracle, to the Spanish mind—had favored the European invaders. At last it was the Incas' turn. Like a proper puppet, Manco asked Hernando Pizarro's permission to conduct ceremonies with Villac Umu in the Yucay valley northwest of Cuzco. He promised to return with a life-size golden statue of Huayna Capac, his father. Hernando's greed undermined his judgment. He let Manco go.

Manco and the high priest promptly joined a war council of chieftains in the mountains; all swore allegiance to Manco and determined to exterminate the Viracochas.

When Manco failed to return to Cuzco, and attack on the capital seemed probable, Hernando confessed his error to his countrymen, horrifying them. They numbered only 190, a force comparable to that which had taken Cajamarca. Only 80 had mounts.

Francisco Pizarro, the Governor of Peru, was contentedly developing Lima, his new capital on the coast. Belated news of the uprisings killed his hopes that the Incas—who had seemed so easily bent to his will—would remain passive. He now regretted that he had tried to stem the arrival of more conquistadors in Peru and had encouraged his partner, Diego de Almagro, to march off to Chile at the head of 570 Spaniards.

Inca insurgents, manning the passes and narrow defiles, cut communication between Cuzco and the coast. Tens of thousands of Inca farmer-warriors marched toward the capital and laid siege. Others captured Spanish settlers, prospectors, and travelers and sent several of their severed heads to Cuzco. Highland peoples revolted everywhere except far to the north, where war weariness

Empire

Massive stone ramparts of Sacsahuaman fortress course a hilltop above Cuzco. Here, in May 1536, Manco Inca launched a rebellion against the Spanish conquerors who had occupied the capital three years earlier. Manco's armies laid siege to the city and burned it; they kept the Spanish occupation force of 190 men surrounded for almost a year.

and unhappy memories of Inca rule discouraged them from joining Manco's rebellion. His well-coordinated uprising demonstrated that the Inca Empire's sinews remained unsevered and that its people, under new leadership, could shake off the apathy induced by civil war and the European invasion.

A century had passed since Manco's great-grandfather Pachacuti had defended Cuzco against Chanca attack. Pachacuti's victory there had marked the empire's birth. Now the empire grasped at survival. High priest Villac Umu urged immediate attack on Cuzco. But Manco insisted on waiting until he possessed the overwhelming mass necessary to smother the Spaniards. His siege army finally totaled anywhere from 50,000 to 400,000 warriors.

As Manco's soldiers closed in, they taunted the Spaniards by lifting their bare legs — an insulting gesture still used in the Andes to provoke fights. They had devised tactics to neutralize cavalry: keeping to the heights, building wicker barriers across streets, lining large pitfalls with sharp stakes, and digging small holes to break horses' legs.

Hurtling down the steeps of Sacsahuaman into the city, warriors fired Cuzco's thatch with red-hot slingstones, setting their capital ablaze and blackening it — even Spaniards later mourned the handsome city's ruination. Advancing like game beaters, attackers crowded many smoke-dazed, choking Europeans into a hall on Cuzco's great square. Miraculously, the fire in its thatch died out, sparing the Spaniards from incineration. A religious painting in Cuzco shows the Virgin Mary extinguishing the flames. Even the Indians came to believe that it had been a miracle.

In house-to-house fighting, Inca troops darted along the sooty tops of roofless walls to avoid being ridden down in Cuzco's narrow streets. They filled the air with large slingstones, twice the size of hens' eggs. The Spaniards would have been overrun except for the brave stand of their Indian auxiliaries, who numbered in the hundreds.

As always, the Spanish defense was furious attack. Day after day, cavalrymen boldly rode out of Cuzco into the midst of the Inca force. They unnerved Indians during the siege by butchering women and hacking off the right hands of captive warriors. To loosen the Inca grip on Cuzco, the Spaniards had to recapture Sacsahuaman, Villac Umu's field headquarters. Protecting themselves from missiles by holding shields overhead, they used scaling ladders to climb the ramparts. They retook Sacsahuaman a month after the siege began.

In the assault, an Inca stone struck Juan Pizarro on the head. Before he died, Juan, in his late twenties, made Gonzalo, his youngest brother, the principal heir of a fortune worth several million dollars. He left nothing to his Inca mistress, but provided a dowry for his mestiza daughter, Isabel.

While beleaguered Hernando held on stubbornly in Cuzco, Manco's warriors annihilated every relief column the Governor

Lost empire of the Incas lives again during Inti Raymi, *a festival of music and dancing that honors the Sun. A musician (left), wearing a traditional feathered headdress, waits his turn to perform at the pageant staged each June 24 at Sacsahuaman. He holds a wooden panpipe, an instrument highlanders have played since pre-Inca times, producing haunting five-toned melodies. At the same time, schoolchildren (above) at Rajchi, 75 miles south of Cuzco, interpret through dance a folk tale of Inca conquest. As Roman Catholic holy days merged with Inca festivals, Inti Raymi came to be observed during Corpus Christi. In other cities as far away as Quito and La Paz, Andean peoples celebrate June 24—the Day of Saint John— by jumping over bonfires.*

sent from Lima. Inca troops reclaimed all of the Peru-Bolivia high-lands except Cuzco and the far north. Manco sent his best general to destroy Lima. The general attacked with standards aloft, vowing to drive the Spaniards to their ships and to keep their wives and produce a race of warriors. For almost two weeks, the Inca army enveloped the city.

But Lima lies on flat, open earth. Cavalry charges again routed the Incas, and a lance struck the general from his litter. He, 40 other chiefs, and uncounted warriors fell dead. The highlanders with-drew into the mountains.

Francisco Pizarro sent frantic appeals for help to Spanish colonies elsewhere. He feared that his brothers had perished in Cuzco. After many months, reinforcements arrived from Ecuador, Panama, Nicaragua, and the Caribbean; supplies came from Cortés in Mexico. From Spain the Queen sent 50 arquebusiers and 50 crossbowmen. Manco Inca had awakened the wrath of a global empire, whereas less than four years earlier Atahuallpa had con-fronted a band of only 168 Spanish adventurers—and lost.

To lift the siege of Cuzco, Hernando Pizarro attempted to seize Manco Inca's temple command post in the mountainside fortress of Ollantaytambo. Its ruins still tower over the Urubamba River several hours drive from Cuzco. Spanish cavalry could only assail that half-built temple of pink granite atop Ollantaytambo if they climbed a narrow staircase flanked by 17 steep terraces.

Ranks of warriors on the terraces received the horsemen with a hail of stones; jungle bowmen launched flights of six-foot arrows. Some Incas donned Spanish helmets, and others tried to fire cap-tured muskets. Manco Inca himself commanded from horseback, wielding a lance. Hernando Pizarro retreated to Cuzco in dismay.

Yet gradually the siege of Cuzco slackened. Sue and I dis-cussed the reasons one day with Dr. Luis A. Pardo, our historian friend. The lives of Manco's men, he explained, followed set pat-terns. "They attacked only at full moon, when the Spaniards could easily detect them. The Incas reserved the dark nights of the new moon for ceremonial dance and ritual intoxication. Many Indians left the siege for sowing and harvest. The Spaniards, however, bound by no such routine, attacked viciously. Also, Manco Inca's great rebellion failed in the end because of bitter memories. Many Indians hated the Incas worse than the Spaniards. Great chiefs with large contingents passed to the Spanish side."

The yearlong siege of Cuzco ended when Almagro and his army returned, bitterly disappointed, from their Chilean expedi-tion. They had wasted a year and a half searching for riches in "New Toledo." Almagro claimed that Cuzco was included in his allotted share—the southern half—of the Inca Empire. He scattered the Indians under Manco, seized the city, and imprisoned the Pizarro brothers—thus precipitating another civil war in Peru. This time it pitted Spaniard against Spaniard: Almagro's "Men of Chile" against the Pizarrist faction.

Almagro held Cuzco and the highlands for a year. He released Hernando Pizarro, and Gonzalo escaped; both joined the Governor on the coast. There Francisco Pizarro assembled troops sent from overseas in answer to his appeal for help in putting down Manco's

Overtaken by conquest, temple walls of pink granite stand unfinished at Ollantaytambo. Hoping to capture Manco here, Hernando Pizarro marched against this cliff-top fortress. Spaniards met a deluge of sling-stones, arrows, and boulders—and retreated to Cuzco. Manco established a jungle state in the mountains of Vilcabamba beyond the fortress.

insurrection. Presently Hernando assumed command and led them against Almagro's Men of Chile.

When he neared Cuzco, Indians gathered in anticipation of a duel between steel-clad Spanish armies. At sunrise on April 26, 1538, rows of mounted knights with shields and lances faced each other across the field of honor. Bugles sounded. Cavalry charged, colliding with a shock that shattered lances and unhorsed riders, to the spectators' delight. Falconets boomed. Infantrymen fired arquebuses loaded with split bullets linked together by iron wire —a European innovation in armament. Indian warriors of both sides fought with star-headed maces.

The soldier-chronicler Cieza tersely described such warfare: "Swords clashed down on helmets, stunning their wearers, and cut through coats of mail; then, pausing for a short space, apart, men glared at each other like bulls in the rutting season."

The civil war abated with the Pizarrist faction supreme. In Cuzco, Hernando Pizarro condemned to death Diego de Almagro, his brother's partner in the pact for conquest made in Panama years earlier. The 63-year-old Almagro besought Hernando "to spare his gray hairs," then fatalistically settled his affairs. He submitted without resistance to the garrote. Many of his followers were banished from Cuzco.

Paullu Inca, brother of Atahuallpa and Manco, had been set up as a puppet ruler. A commander of native troops in Almagro's Chilean expedition, he resisted Manco's entreaties to join the continuing rebellion against Spanish rule. Paullu took up residence in Manco Capac's palace. He received a Spanish coat of arms, and priests baptized his dozens of children. He controlled vast numbers of farms throughout the empire.

To rid Cuzco of unruly Spanish soldiers, Hernando Pizarro encouraged expeditions of exploration. Hundreds of Spaniards and thousands of Indians died in the eastern jungles.

His siege of Cuzco a failure, Manco Inca took to roving the central Andes of Peru, provoking uprisings and killing Spanish travelers. Cornered one day with 80 followers, he and three chieftains, mounted on captured horses and brandishing lances, rode down an astonished force of 30 Spanish foot soldiers who had tried to seize him. He and his chieftains, backed by warriors armed with maces, killed 24, and mauled the rest.

On another front—southern Peru and Bolivia—the warlike high priest Villac Umu spread terror. Eventually his uprisings were put down by Hernando and Gonzalo Pizarro. Paullu Inca fought beside them, with fine generalship. Sword in hand, he even wounded some of his own Indians because they fled. Spaniards said that Paullu was unbelievably loyal to the crown.

Manco Inca, Paullu's brother, remained equally loyal to the Indian cause. Manco never gave up, but Spanish arms and cruel reprisals countered each of his revolts. Some of his captains were captured; others surrendered—even Villac Umu. Manco finally

Surprised by assassins in his palace at Lima, 63-year-old Francisco Pizarro fights to the death. Dispossessed followers of Almagro, who had plotted for months, killed the conquistador in his chambers in 1541.

established a new Inca capital in Vilcabamba, northwest of Cuzco, an almost impenetrable Amazon headwater region of lightning-slashed snows and snake-ridden quagmires.

Governor Pizarro sought to win Manco over with diplomacy. The fifteenth Inca responded by killing the Governor's representatives. Furious, Pizarro had Manco's sister-wife stripped, tied to a tree, scourged with rods, and shot to death with arrows. Then he floated her body downriver in a basket into the Inca camp. Next, he burned alive Villac Umu and 15 other Inca captains who had trusted his promises.

Hernando Pizarro returned to Spain, ready to hang up his sword but apprehensive about reprisals for Almagro's execution. His worry proved well founded. Charles I ordered him confined to the Castle La Mota, northwest of Madrid. There he would spend two decades—most pleasantly. With his New World riches, Hernando set himself up in luxury. In 1552 he married his niece Francisca, a daughter of Francisco Pizarro by a sister of Atahuallpa, thus adding her huge fortune to his own. Hernando was the only Pizarro to make it back to Spain. He died there in 1578, aged nearly 80.

For capturing the rich Inca Empire and holding fast during the rebellion, Charles I gave Francisco Pizarro the title of marquis. Still, the ghost of Almagro lingered: His dispossessed Men of Chile plotted revenge. Pizarro scoffed, waving away warnings of assassination. In Lima, after Mass one Sunday in 1541, armed men burst into his palace. Some of Pizarro's companions jumped out windows. His half-brother Martín de Alcántara died fighting the assassins.

Sixty-three-year-old Francisco Pizarro struggled valiantly. The Marquis took the measure of three conspirators before a sword point pierced his throat. That night the conqueror of Peru was buried by candlelight in an obscure corner of a church.

Bishop Valverde of Cuzco—the friar who had baptized Atahuallpa—fled when he learned of Pizarro's fate. He got as far as Ecuador. On Puná, near the place where he had first set foot in the land of the Incas, Valverde was killed by cannibals.

Seven renegade Men of Chile took refuge with Manco Inca in the wilds of Vilcabamba. He befriended them and bade them teach his guerrillas Spanish tactics and use of weapons. The outlaws stayed two years. Then, when the first Spanish viceroy landed in 1544, they sought to gain favor with him. One of the conspirators who had killed Francisco Pizarro now joined in stabbing Manco Inca in the back during a game of quoits. Manco survived long enough to name his five-year-old son, Sayri Tupa Inca, as heir.

For nine full years Manco had held out. He had lived up to his lordly name: Manco Inca Yupanqui. A descendant of emperors, so highborn that his marriage was legalized by the Pope, he had remained true to his heritage though it finally came down to plotting insurrection in a wild and bat-infested jungle. After Manco died, his nobles abandoned his innovative ways. Their remote kingdom remained inviolate.

Murky Amazon tributary winds through treacherous wilderness in eastern Peru. Hundreds of Spaniards and thousands of Indian warriors and bearers died searching the jungle for nonexistent cities of gold.

Gonzalo Pizarro, appointed Governor of Quito, had ventured into the jungle east of Ecuador's volcanoes in quest of cinnamon and cities of gold. With 220 Spaniards, 4,000 Indians, and thousands of hogs, llamas, and dogs, he entered the steaming morass in February 1541, but did not reach the confluence of the Coca and Napo Rivers—only 100 miles away—until Christmas. His retinue was reduced to eating dogs and precious horses. In the search for food, Gonzalo sent a party of foragers downriver under one-eyed Francisco de Orellana, who went on to become the first explorer to descend the Amazon. This river possibly took its name from skirted warriors like the "Black Amazons" of *Amadís.*

When Gonzalo Pizarro slogged home to Quito hollow-eyed and empty-handed, he found the realm in chaos and his brother Francisco dead a year. The ambitious Gonzalo eventually became ruler of all the lands that once comprised the Inca Empire except the little Inca state of Vilcabamba. His power grew out of his opposition to Spanish edicts.

Published protests of Friar Bartolomé de las Casas, later Bishop and "Apostle of the Indies," and other staunch friends of the Indians, had aroused moral indignation in Spain over the fate of native Americans. And the "New Laws" of 1542 were designed to curtail holdings of settlers and to prohibit abuse of Indians; the viceroy in Peru, Blasco Núñez Vela, who arrived in 1544, was charged with enforcing those laws.

New World Spaniards were outraged. They had not come to grub the land, tend sheep, or labor in the mines. This they could have done in Spain. But now that the gold of the Incas was gone, old warriors and new arrivals could only aspire to the control of natives who would work the land and pay tribute: the old system of *encomienda* inherited from Spain.

Gonzalo Pizarro, richest man in Peru, opposed the New Laws. Conquistadors and settlers alike flocked to his standard. The proud young warlord with the famous name, veteran of Cajamarca, Jauja, Cuzco, Bolivia's conquest, and the Amazon jungle, led a force that killed the new viceroy in a battle at Añaquito, north of Quito. Later, Gonzalo defeated a royalist force at Huarina, a community on the southeastern shore of Lake Titicaca. He ruled for almost four years, a dictator in open rebellion against Charles, King of Spain and head of the Holy Roman Empire.

Then King Charles sent a royal emissary with full imperial powers: Pedro de la Gasca, an ecclesiastic who sought to win back the disaffected Spaniards by repealing the New Laws. La Gasca raised an army and advanced into the highlands, looking for Gonzalo. His army grew stronger with each battle as Spaniards switched over to the King's side.

The final encounter between La Gasca and Pizarro took place at Xaquixaguana near Cuzco's western approaches, the site of so much mayhem in the century since Pachacuti flayed the defeated Chancas. There, less than 15 years earlier, Pizarro had seen Chalcuchima, Atahuallpa's general, burned at the stake.

The soldier-chronicler Cieza lost some notebooks in that last skirmish, which never developed into a battle. Gonzalo Pizarro, mounted on a spirited chestnut horse and wearing fine armor

Rainbow-tinted clouds etch the horizon at dawn beyond a fleet of fishing balsas moored on the Bolivian shore of Lake Titicaca. Indians still build these craft as in Inca times, lashing together bundles of totora, hollow reeds that flourish along the fringes of the lake. An Aymara Indian (left) puts finishing touches on the stern of a new balsa. Bulky, but easy to paddle or sail, the boats stay afloat for as long as a year, gradually rotting and becoming waterlogged. Lakeshore peoples use totora in many other ways: for food, furniture, fish traps and floats, matting for walls and floors, thatch for roofing, fuel for cooking, and fodder for cattle.

inlaid with gold, urged his comrades on — only to watch in consternation as one after another deserted to the King's standard.

The last of the Pizarro brothers in the New World surrendered and La Gasca had him beheaded next day.

With Gonzalo perished his chief tactician and executioner, Francisco de Carbajal. The murderous 84-year-old conquistador had just begun making a fortune in silver in Bolivia — a much surer enterprise than questing for cities of gold.

The richest silver lode on earth, a mountain of it, had been discovered at Potosí, Bolivia, 300 miles southeast of Lake Titicaca, in 1545; Almagro had unwittingly passed it by on his fruitless search for treasure in the southern half of the Inca Empire. The lode laced a 15,827-foot cone dominating a bleak and twisted landscape of tawny rock too high for much vegetation. In time, Potosí produced billions of dollars worth of silver to help finance Spain's imperial adventures. To extract it, countless Indians of Collasuyu — the southeast quarter of the Inca world — sweated and died inside the chambered mountain.

As the supply of miners became depleted, others were conscripted from Peru and Argentina by a Spanish adaptation of the mita, the Incas' obligatory labor stint. They came from districts up to three months' journey distant. From one area alone, a total of about 7,000 workers and members of their families and 40,000 animals, mostly llamas, were sent yearly to Potosí.

On every shift, around 4,500 Indians descended wobbly rawhide ladders down a 750-foot vertical shaft into a honeycomb of tunnels. There they toiled in foul air by the flicker of tallow candles. Each bearer carried as much as 100 pounds of ore on his back up the ladders. Underground tours of duty increased from eight hours to six full days. Narcotic coca leaves, once reserved for Inca royalty, dulled pain and hunger; coca became the leading cash crop of the viceroyalty.

Outside, thousands more laborers worked sluices, waterwheels, grinding mills, and settling basins in which mercury absorbed silver from crushed ore. Kilns then vaporized mercury from the precious metal. The quicksilver came from mines in Huancavelica, far to the north in Peru, where untold numbers of Indians agonized and died of mercury poisoning.

Sue and I journeyed to Potosí, one of the most remote and lofty cities ever populated by Western man. We found it spent from its exciting trajectory to become, more than three centuries ago, the largest city in the New World. Then, its population was 160,000 — almost equal to Venice's. Now, Potosí counts about one-third that many residents. Rain splashes through rotting roofs of churches and dribbles over huge sooty paintings hanging awry on adobe walls. Little trace remains of the old city's eight fencing schools and 36 gaming houses. But we did lean on a balcony of a ballroom where, in 1616, the year Shakespeare, Cervantes, and Garcilaso died, ladies of Potosí danced in the rarefied air at 13,000 feet. They wore silks from Cathay and pearls from Isla de Margarita, off Venezuela's coast.

The rustle of silk is gone, but the chatter of woolen-shawled women in the marketplace goes on as before. The silver lodes are

Bent to her task, a street cleaner sweeps a curb in Potosí, Bolivia, once the mining capital of the New World. Founded in 1545 by followers of Pizarro, Potosí soon burgeoned into a Spanish-flavored metropolis of casinos, fencing schools, ballrooms, a cathedral, and a mint. To extract ore, Indians toiled in weeklong shifts in hot, dark, and noxious tunnels.

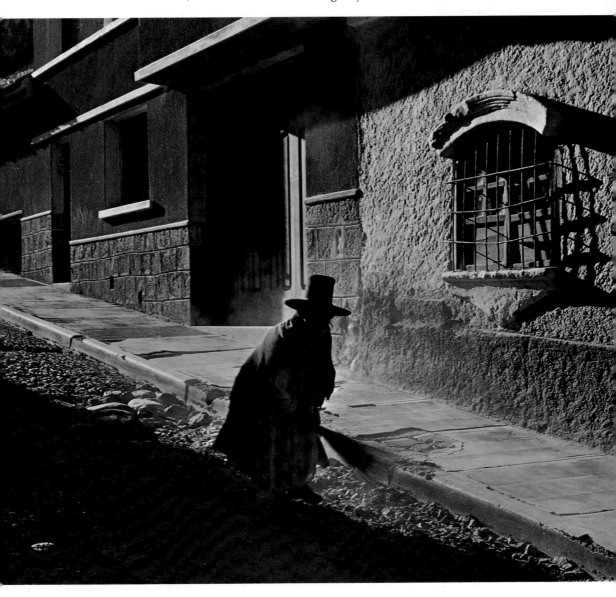

Christian fervor burns in the faces of Andean worshipers during religious observances. Spanish missionaries, accompanying conquistadors who marched across Inca lands in search of gold, preached Christian gospel. Although the Incas relinquished their gold, they clung to the religion of their ancestors; but in time nearly all Andean people accepted Roman Catholicism. During Corpus Christi, parishioners in Cuzco shoulder an image of La Virgen de Belén for a procession from Almuden Church (right) to the Church of Bethlehem; there (below left), worshipers place candles under the statue. One supplicant at a festival near Cuzco symbolically relives the suffering of Christ by wearing a crown of thorns; another in Ecuador holds a coin-studded rosary.

Shielding his pregnant wife, Tupa Amaru, Manco Inca's son, surrenders to Spanish captors. Viceroy Francisco de Toledo, vowing to destroy the Inca dynasty, pursued young Tupa Amaru deep into the jungle.

exhausted, and now the acrid smell of sulphur from processed tin pervades the streets. The mountain is almost hollowed out; its entrails clog the valleys. Old women in black witch-like hats sift through the tailings, gleaning chunks of tin ore.

King Charles I tried to correct New World wrongs. In 1550 he even ordered an end to military conquest of overseas "naturals" until theologians and imperial counselors could decide whether it was just. But ruffians in the Indies ignored the faraway voice of Europe's strongest ruler. Compassionate Spanish writers protested the mita, the conditions in the mines, illegal demands for Indian tribute and porterage, and abuses by Spaniards and selfish Indian leaders. They objected vigorously to corrupt magistrates and *encomenderos* who enslaved tenants, exacted excessive tribute, and haughtily rode in Inca-style litters. By royal edict, encomenderos were supposed to leave the Indians alone.

To the credit of the Spanish conscience, such vehement protests received wide circulation. But one illustrated critique of New World times came to light only in 1908: the 1,179-page *Nueva Corónica y Buen Gobierno—New Chronicle and Good Government—*penned by Indian satirist Felipe Guamán Poma de Ayala. In mixed Spanish, Quechua, and other Andean tongues, Guamán Poma—"Hawk Puma"—depicted a coarse world hardly recognizable as the same one that "El Inca" Garcilaso was describing so smoothly about the same time: the end of the 16th and the beginning of the 17th centuries.

Guamán Poma was a minor official of the province of the Rucanas—litter bearers to the Incas—west of Cuzco. In hundreds of one-page essays and 397 illustrations, he poured out his Christian concern about the condition of the Indians—to him so bad that "to write it is to cry." By the standards of "don Felipe," the Incas were despotic usurpers given to child sacrifice. Manco Capac, the founding father, he called a whoreson. The Spaniards, he said, were worse.

He wrote a Quechua prayer for the Indians: "From fire, water, earthquake free me Jesus Christ. . . . from authorities, magistrates . . . priests, from all the gentlemen, thieves . . . free me Jesus Christ from those who raise false testimony, from haters, men or women, from drunks, from those who do not fear God and justice."

Authorities threw agitator Guamán Poma out of his highland home. In Lima he worked on his book; its illustrations have come down to us as the only pictorial record of his times. Guamán Poma wrote poor history but produced an amazing social tract, though its documentation was biased and confined to the narrow region along the Cuzco-Lima highway that he traveled. The Incas had prohibited aimless travel, but now, to escape taxation, many Indians left their farms and wandered the chaotic land.

Guamán Poma called the Spaniards "deportees from Castile" and the Negroes "deportees from Guinea," wishing both to go back whence they came. People of mixed blood—mestizos and mulattoes—were "fine for the galleys," he wrote. He worried, in his words, that "Indians will be wiped out."

Friar Valverde, the priest at Atahuallpa's capture and later Bishop of Cuzco, had first warned of genocide in 1539. Spanish viceroys later echoed him. War, plague, and loss of the will to live by effacement of dignity cut Indian population drastically. From the conquest to Guamán Poma's day, the population had diminished by three-fourths. "All will end mestizos," the Indian satirist predicted.

Today, mestizos *are* numerically dominant in the Four Quarters of the World. They flock to the cities, contributing to the urban population explosion. But

Tupa Amaru, the last Inca, walks in chains to Cuzco in this drawing by Indian chronicler Felipe Guamán Poma de Ayala. Toledo had the Inca beheaded there in 1572—horrifying Indians and Spaniards alike.

most pure Indians dwell where their ancestors fled for survival in the 16th century: deep in the mountains, where springs and caves and odd-shaped pebbles still hold magic.

Survival for Paullu Inca, last of Huayna Capac's male progeny, meant serving the Spanish cause unswervingly. Paullu's son Carlos Inca grew up among the mestizo sons of the conquistadors and married a Spanish lady from the Pizarros' hometown, Trujillo, Spain. Carlos Inca's will disposed of numerous encomiendas but left no hint of his Inca origins.

Survival for the sons of Manco Inca meant hiding out in the Inca state of Vilcabamba. The son that Manco named Inca before he died, Sayri Tupa Inca, was lured out of Vilcabamba when he came of age and the Pope confirmed his marriage to his sister. After many anguished auguries, the old regents had concurred with his decision to leave the jungle. The sacred forehead fringe of office went to his more capable brother, Titu Cusi.

Vilcabamba carried on despite scanty manpower and limited agriculture and the fact that almost all Indians were passively or actively aiding the Spaniards. The little state's security lay in the enveloping jungle beyond the beloved highlands. Titu Cusi, the mercurial son of Manco Inca, kept Vilcabamba alive 13 more years through negotiations with the Spaniards. He cut back on guerrilla attacks and accepted missionaries.

Titu Cusi always seemed about to give himself up — but never did. His priests performed the old rites to the Sun. His bodyguards were jungle cannibals. Whenever emissaries came from Cuzco, Inca warriors in colored masks, golden breastplates, and feather ornaments met them at suspension bridges.

To finish off the Incas became the avowed personal goal of Viceroy Francisco de Toledo, who landed in Peru in 1569. The Crown, now in the person of Philip II, granted him absolute power to restore good government. Toledo, a superb administrator, had strong opinions on how to go about it.

First he toured the royal roads gathering *Informaciones* — they would become historic — from old chieftains to discredit the Incas. He ascertained that the Inca Empire had lasted barely a century and that some tribes hated Inca overlords. His zealous aides rooted out native sorcerers and priests and burned thousands of idols, mummies, and quipus. He ordered Indians brought from the hills, settled in villages, and instructed in moral behavior.

Then Toledo abruptly banished from Cuzco the rich puppet Incas and took over their encomiendas. And he raised an army to obliterate Vilcabamba.

Well-armed colonial gentlemen of Cuzco, supported by a thousand local Indians and 500 Cañaris from Ecuador, plunged into Vilcabamba. Inca defectors guided them. Indian defense proved no better than in 1532; Inca generals had abandoned Manco's teachings of Spanish tactics.

The Indians set fire to their stores and palaces and slipped away. Toledo's men entered Vilcabamba's smoldering capital on June 24, 1572. Nearby they found the body of a martyred missionary and, in the ashes, two mummies: Manco Inca and his son Titu Cusi, who had died a year earlier.

Another son of Manco, Tupa Amaru, had been designated Inca. With the fall of Vilcabamba, he escaped into the jungle. Spaniards pursued him downriver by raft and in forced marches by torchlight, and found him huddled by a campfire with his pregnant wife. They also captured a long-sought image of the Sun, the Punchao: a gold idol filled with the dust of dead Incas' hearts.

Viceroy Toledo ordered young Tupa Amaru's execution, despite supplications from horrified Spaniards. Thousands of Indians gathered to witness and bewail the dire event. In the great square of Cuzco, a Cañari swordsman beheaded the last Inca — 39 years after Atahuallpa was garroted in Cajamarca.

Wearing red forehead fringe—the crown of Inca emperors—and a sun
disk on his chest, a latter-day "Inca" leads the Catholic procession of
Corpus Christi through Cuzco's streets in this 17th-century painting.

The repercussions of this act still echo. They were felt when Toledo returned to Spain after setting up a colonial system that would endure two centuries. King Philip threw him out of the palace, saying that he had been sent to serve kings, not to kill them. In the 1780's, José Gabriel Tupa Amaru—a great-great-great-grandson of the last Inca—spearheaded an uprising that spread from Cuzco as far as Argentina. He was captured and—with all his family—horribly mutilated in Cuzco's plaza. Revolutionaries who freed Argentina from Spain early in the 1800's considered seeking out a descendant of Tupa Amaru to become monarch. In the 1960's, Uruguayan urban terrorists took the name Tupamaru. The Peruvian government in the 1970's adopted a stylized image of José Gabriel Tupa Amaru as a symbol of social reform.

After the beheading of the last Inca, jungle gradually engulfed Vilcabamba. Roots and buttresses of towering trees pried open the temples. Soil reclaimed stone. The rain-forest canopy spread over the last bastion of the Inca Empire. And centuries passed.

Then, in 1909, explorer Hiram Bingham, attracted to the Apurímac gorge by archeologist E. George Squier's drawing of the chasm's great suspension bridge, was invited by Peruvian treasure seekers to investigate an Inca ruin—possibly the lost capital. He found only an outpost, but his zest for further quest was fired.

Two years later Bingham returned. He penetrated the Vilcabamba region and discovered one ancient ruin after another. Near uncharted mountains reaching to 20,000 feet, his Indian guides finally halted at Inca buildings in the jungle lowlands near Espíritu Pampa—Plain of Ghosts. Was this Manco Inca's capital of Vilcabamba? Bingham decided not: The area was too hot and humid, too enervating for highlanders. There were too few ruins. Because his guides feared attack by jungle bowmen, he turned back.

Had Bingham pressed on a few yards farther, he would have discovered acres of buildings in the forest—almost certainly Vilcabamba. In 1964, another American, Gene Savoy, retraced Bingham's trail, took those extra steps, and was astounded by the rambling Inca city.

At the outset of that 1911 expedition, Hiram Bingham *did* make a spectacular find—which he recorded in *Lost City of the Incas*—that has enriched the lives of all who have seen it. It now brings into Peru tourist wealth greater than all the gold in Atahuallpa's ransom. The find cost Bingham half a day and half a dollar.

Instead of following the route described by chroniclers, he had taken a road recently blasted from cliffs along the Urubamba River gorge below Ollantaytambo. He inquired about ruins as he went. On the sixth night out of Cuzco, he camped by the hut of an Indian who mentioned that farmers were cultivating terraces on "very good ruins" nearby. "I offered to pay him well if he would show me the ruins. He demurred . . . it was too hard a climb," wrote Bingham. "But when he found that I was willing to pay . . . fifty cents . . . three or four times the ordinary daily wage . . . he finally

Relics of a plundered empire, skulls and bones cover an ancient cemetery near Lima. Much of the Inca heritage has disappeared through looting—beginning with the conquest and continuing to the present.

Overleaf: Mountain-locked citadel of Machu Picchu clings to a jungle crag in Peru. Discovered in 1911, this Inca settlement remains a puzzle; no clear record exists of its origin or the reason for its abandonment.

Dusk touches Machu Picchu's sacred Inti Huatana, *the Incas' "hitching post of the Sun." Spaniards toppled such religious symbols, and the Sun God wandered—leaving the empire of the Incas in darkness.*

agreed to go. When asked just where the ruins were, he pointed straight up to the top of the mountain."

Within a few hours Bingham and his guide had scaled a precipitous 2,000-foot slope, aided by primitive ladders of notched logs. At the top, two smiling farmers who "enjoyed being free" from tax collectors sent a little boy to guide him. The child led the explorer along rockwork partly concealed beneath trees and moss —the growth of centuries, Bingham said. Then came revelation: "... the work of a master artist.... Surprise followed surprise in bewildering succession. We came to a great stairway.... The sight held me spellbound.... the principal temple.... Would anyone believe what I had found?"

Hiram Bingham had discovered Machu Picchu, the most spectacular sanctuary of the Inca Empire undefiled by conquerors. No specific mention of this cliff-top citadel surrounded on three sides by the gigantic moat of the Urubamba appears in the chronicles. The earliest reference Bingham found was dated 1875.

Sue and I made our own discovery of Machu Picchu in 1948, when visitors still climbed the cliff on muleback. In 1954, while filming for a week at the then-tiny hostel, only two other tourists joined me. Now daily jets fly throngs of many nationalities to Cuzco, and hundreds make the train ride down the magnificent Urubamba gorge to discover a lost city of the Incas for themselves.

What was Machu Picchu? Conjectures range widely: birthplace of the Inca Empire; a military outpost; capital of Vilcabamba; an imperial retreat; a refuge for Virgins of the Sun; ceremonial center of a network of settlements.

To experience the almost spiritual bewitchment of Machu Picchu, Sue and I have sometimes stayed to witness sunset and sunrise from a crag overlooking the temples and terraces. And I have wished aloud that I could travel back in time to visit this mysterious citadel in the sky in its days of grandeur. But Sue replies, "I like it just as it is ... as if held in a magic spell."

The enchantment of the Incas' timeless land tightens its bonds on me when I follow barelegged Indian porters over mountain passes higher than llamas graze. At sundown we take refuge in a smoky hut and the wiry little men share with me a thick soup of charqui and chuño—dehydrated meat and potatoes such as sustained Inca armies on the march.

An eerie feeling like the glacial chill of Andean night creeps down my spine when they—the elders, especially—call me "Viracocha." That is the name the troubled citizens of Cuzco gave the Spaniards in 1532; in remote places white men are still so addressed, although use of the title recalls a terrible mistake.

For I am not—nor was there ever—a fair god from over the sea sent by the Incas' supreme being, Viracocha, to save their empire.

Index

Boldface indicates illustrations;
italic refers to picture captions.

Acknowledgments

The Special Publications Division is grateful to the individuals and institutions named or quoted in the text and to those cited here for their generous cooperation and assistance during the preparation of this book: Embassies of Argentina, Bolivia, Brazil, Chile, Colombia, Ecuador, and Peru; the National Arboretum, the Smithsonian Institution, and the United States Department of State.

Additional Reading

Eugenio Alarco, *El Hombre Peruano en Su Historia;* Miriam Beltrán, *Cuzco, Window on Peru;* Wendell C. Bennett, *Ancient Arts of the Andes;* Hiram Bingham, *Inca Land* and *Lost City of the Incas;* Burr C. Brundage, *Lords of Cuzco;* G. H. S. Bushnell, *Peru;* Pedro de Cieza de León, *Chronicle of Peru* and *Civil Wars of Peru* (Chupas, La Salinas, and Quito); Bernabé Cobo, *Historia del Nuevo Mundo;* Lieselotte and Theo Engl, *Twilight of Ancient Peru;* Paul Fejos, *Archeological Explorations in the Cordillera Vilcabamba, Southeastern Peru;* Bertrand Flornoy, *The World of the Inca;* Garcilaso de la Vega, *Royal Commentaries of the Incas and General History of Peru;* Felipe Guamán Poma de Ayala, *Nueva Corónica y Buen Gobierno;* Lewis Hanke, *The Spanish Struggle for Justice in the Conquest of America;* John Hemming, *The Conquest of the Incas;* Thor Heyerdahl, *American Indians in the Pacific;* Hammond Innes, *The Conquistadors;* F. A. Kirkpatrick, *The Spanish Conquistadores;* Paul Kosok, *Life, Land and Water in Ancient Peru;* Weston La Barre, *The Aymara Indians of the Lake Titicaca Plateau, Bolivia;* Edward P. Lanning, *Peru Before the Incas;* Rafael Larco Hoyle, *Peru;* James Lockhart, *The Men of Cajamarca* and *Spanish Peru, 1532-1560;* S. K. Lothrop, *Inca Treasure as Depicted by Spanish Historians;* Luis G. Lumbreras, *The Peoples and Cultures of Ancient Peru;* Clements R. Markham, editor, *Narratives of the Rites and Laws of The Yncas;* J. Alden Mason, *The Ancient Civilizations of Peru;* Philip A. Means, *Ancient Civilizations of the Andes, Biblioteca Andina,* and *Fall of the Inca Empire;* Alfred Métraux, *The History of the Incas;* Tony Morrison, *Land Above the Clouds;* Martin de Murúa, *Historia General del Perú;* Pedro Pizarro, *Relation of the Discovery and Conquest of the Kingdoms of Peru;* William H. Prescott, *History of the Conquest of Peru;* John H. Rowe, *Introduction to the Archaeology of Cuzco;* John H. Rowe and Dorothy Menzel, *Peruvian Archaeology;* Pedro Sancho, *An Account of the Conquest of Peru;* Pedro Sarmiento de Gamboa, *Historia de los Incas;* Gene Savoy, *Antisuyo;* William L. Schurz, *This New World;* E. George Squier, *Peru;* Julian H. Steward, editor, *Handbook of South American Indians,* especially Volume II; Victor W. Von Hagen, *Highway of the Sun;* Francisco de Xeres et al., *Reports on the Discovery of Peru;* Agustín de Zárate et al., *The Discovery and Conquest of Peru,* especially the translation by J. M. Cohen. National Geographic books: Helen and Frank Schreider, *Exploring the Amazon;* George E. Stuart, *Discovering Man's Past in the Americas.* Readers may also want to consult the National Geographic Index for related material.

Library of Congress CIP Data

McIntyre, Loren 1917-
    The Incredible Incas and
    Their Timeless Land.
    Bibliography p. 198.
    Includes Index.
    1. Incas. 2. Peru — Antiquities.
3. Peru — Description and travel —
1951-   I. National Geo-
graphic Society, Washington, D. C.
Special Publications Division.
II. Title.
F3429.M18   985'.004'98   74-28805
ISBN 0-87044-177-9

Composition for *The Incredible Incas and
Their Timeless Land* by National Geographic's Phototypographic Division,
Carl M. Shrader, Chief; Lawrence F.
Ludwig, Assistant Chief. Printed and
bound by Fawcett Printing Corp., Rockville, Md. Color separations by Color-
graphics, Inc., Forestville, Md; Graphic
Color Plate, Inc., Stamford, Conn.; The
Lanman Co., Washington, D. C.; Pro-
gressive Color Corp., Rockville, Md.;
and J. Wm. Reed Co., Alexandria, Va.

THE INCA DYNASTY
Circa 1200-1572

Lords of Cuzco

MANCO CAPAC	Son of the Sun, mythical founder of dynasty.
SINCHI ROCA *(son of Manco Capac)*	Designed forehead fringe that denoted royalty.
LLOQUE YUPANQUI *(son of Sinchi Roca)*	Threatened by other tribes coexisting in Cuzco valley, begot late in life.
MAYTA CAPAC *(son of Lloque Yupanqui)*	Child prodigy, Hercules of Inca legend.
CAPAC YUPANQUI *(son of Mayta Capac)*	First to exact tribute from tribes beyond Cuzco valley.
INCA ROCA *(son of Capac Yupanqui)*	Organized schools for boys of imperial class, first to use "Inca" as a noble title.
YAHUAR HUACAC *(son of Inca Roca)*	Kidnaped as a child, cemented relations with neighboring tribes by marriage.
VIRACOCHA *(son of Yahuar Huacac)*	Took name of lord creator, began conquest beyond Cuzco valley.

Emperors of Tahuantinsuyu, Four Quarters of the World

PACHACUTI *(son of Viracocha)*	First emperor, mighty conqueror, creator of the Inca Empire by conquest. 1438-1471
TUPA INCA *(son of Pachacuti)*	Second emperor, one of history's farthest-ranging conquerors. 1471-1493
HUAYNA CAPAC *(son of Tupa Inca)*	Third emperor, expanded empire northward, died of plague amid bad omens. 1493-1527
HUASCAR *(son of Huayna Capac)*	Fourth emperor, overthrown by civil war, executed by Atahuallpa. 1527-1532
ATAHUALLPA *(son of Huayna Capac)*	Captured and executed by Francisco Pizarro. 1532-1533

Incas After the Spanish Conquest

TUPA HUALLPA *(son of Huayna Capac)*	Crowned by Spaniards, possibly poisoned. 1533-1533
MANCO INCA *(son of Huayna Capac)*	Crowned by Spaniards, rebelled in 1536, set up Inca jungle state. 1533-1545
PAULLU INCA *(son of Huayna Capac)*	Puppet Inca, ruled Cuzco, commanded Indian troops supporting Spaniards. 1537-1549
CARLOS INCA *(son of Paullu Inca)*	Puppet Inca, ruled Cuzco, married Spanish lady. 1549-1572
SAYRI TUPA INCA *(first son of Manco Inca)*	Succeeded Manco Inca as ruler of Inca jungle state. 1545-1558
TITU CUSI *(second son of Manco Inca)*	Ruled in Inca jungle state, defied Spaniards. 1558-1571
TUPA AMARU *(third son of Manco Inca)*	Captured in jungle, executed by Spanish viceroy. 1571-1572

Guide to Pronunciation of Inca Names
(accented syllables in all capital letters)

Manco Capac — MAHN-ko KAH-pahk
Sinchi Roca — SIN-chee RO-kah
Lloque Yupanqui — YO-kay Yu-PAHN-kee
Mayta Capac — MAHY-ta KAH-pahk
Capac Yupanqui — KAH-pahk Yu-PAHN-kee
Inca Roca — IN-kah RO-kah
Yahuar Huacac — YAH-war WAH-kahk
Viracocha — Wir-ah-KO-chah
Pachacuti — Pah-chah-KOO-tee
Tupa Inca — TU-pah IN-kah

Huayna Capac — WAHY-nah KAH-pahk
Huascar — WAHS-kar
Atahuallpa — Ah-tah-WAHL-pah
Tupa Huallpa — TU-pah WAHL-pah
Manco Inca — MAHN-ko IN-kah
Paullu Inca — POWL-yu IN-kah
Carlos Inca — CAR-los IN-kah
Sayri Tupa Inca — SAHY-ree TU-pah IN-kah
Titu Cusi — TEE-too KOO-see
Tupa Amaru — TU-pah Ah-MAH-roo

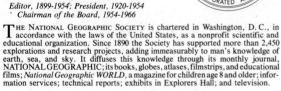